ALBERT QUIXALL

- THE GOLDEN BOY OF MANCHESTER UNITED AND SHEFFIELD WEDNESDAY

Albert Quixall

The Golden Boy of Manchester United and Sheffield Wednesday

Iain McCartney

Copyright © Iain McCartney 2025
The moral rights of the author have been asserted.

www.1889books.co.uk
ISBN: 978-1-915045-49-2

Other publications by Iain McCartney

Duncan Edwards: Black Country Boy to Red Devil, (co-authored with Roy Kavanagh), Temple Publishing, 1999
Roger Byrne – Captain of the Busby Babes, Empire Publishing, 2000
Old Trafford: 100 Years of the Theatre of Dreams, Yore Publishing, 2010
Building the Dynasty: Manchester United 1946-1958, Pitch Publishing, 2015
Manchester United: Rising from the Wreckage 1958-68, Amberley Publishing, 2013
Manchester United: Busby's Legacy, Amberley Publishing, 2014
The Tartan Reds, Britespot Publishing Ltd, 2002
Irish Reds, Britespot Publishing Ltd, 2002
Duncan Edwards: The Full Report, Empire Publications, 2012
Manchester United: The Forgotten Fixtures, Breedon Books Publishing Co Ltd, 2009
Manchester United: Thirty Memorable Games from the Fifties, JMD Media Ltd, 2013
Manchester United : Thirty Memorable Games from the Sixties, JMD Media Ltd, 2012
Manchester United – 100 Facts, Wymer Publishing, 2017
Old Trafford: 100 Years of the Theatre of Dreams, Empire Publications, 2010
The Official Manchester United Players' A-Z, Simon & Schuster UK, 2013
George Best Fifty Defining Fixtures, Amberley Publishing, 2015
Sir Alex Ferguson: Fifty Defining Fixtures, Amberley Publishing, 2013
Manchester United's first FA Cup Success in 1909: Remembering that first time, JMD Media Ltd, 2012
Duncan Edwards: Black Country Boy to Red Devil, (co-authored with Jim Cadman), Cornerstone Marketing Limited, 2018
The United Tour of Manchester, (co-authored with Tom Clare), Amberley Publishing, 2013
Manchester United Collectibles, Amberley Publishing, 2018
Manchester United: Ten Days in May: The Class of '63, Legends Publishing, 2022
Ernest Mangnall: The Architect of Mancunian Football, Empire Publications, 2022
John Henry Davies: King Midas, Empire Publications, 2024
Queen of the South: The History: The History 1919-2008, DB Publishing, 2013
Soul in Print: A History of Soul Fanzines and Magazines, New Haven Publishing Ltd, 2021
The Four Tops, New Haven Publishing Ltd, 2024
David Halliday – The Forgotten Legend, Self-published, 2020
A History of the Dumfries Music Scene, Self-published

Best wishes
Albert [signature]

CONTENTS

1. From Schoolboy to Owlet   1
2. The Only Way is Up   26
3. Wednesday, The Army and England at Last   44
4. Relegation and Resurgence   60
5. Enough is Enough   76
6. Aboard the United Rollercoaster   100
7. All That Glitters is not Gold   122
8. Those Twilight Years   135
9. My Dad   141

CHAPTER ONE
FROM SCHOOLBOY TO OWLET

Albert Quixall was a pioneer of the modern game. His quiff and Billy Fury looks made him identifiable to that new phenomenon: the teenager. He was literally one of the first proper poster-boys of the game, his face adorning many a bedroom wall. He had a rebel streak, wore his shorts shockingly short compared to the old guard, styled his hair as opposed to slicking it down with Brylcreem. Like a Beckham of his day, his name filled column inches and his "golden-boy" footballing career fuelled speculation and sold newspapers. His record transfer fee of £45,000 in 1958 brought him under an intense spotlight, and added pressure to a star who never quite lived up to the hype.

But as well as the stardom and glamour, tragedy is woven into the life of Albert Quixall, from both a personal and professional viewpoint. The death of two family members, one that he would have known little about, would have tugged at the heart strings, while the Munich air disaster of February 1958 was to bring grief from the professional point of view, with the loss of opponents, who had become friends.

There was also the personal tragedy in latter years, brought on by his health, one opponent that Albert Quixall could not overcome.

The first of those unexpected tragedy's came on August 28th 1938, when his uncle, George Quixall, his father's brother, died in Sheffield Royal Infirmary, never having regained consciousness, hours after having been admitted with numerous injuries, including a fractured skull, following a motor-cycle accident. Riding as the pillion passenger, the motor-cycle was in collision with a telegraph pole in Ecclesfield, as George and his friend, John Lane, were returning home after attending a dance at Chapeltown.

This was followed in 1950, when his grandfather, also George Quixall, died at St James Park as he watched his beloved Sheffield Wednesday play Newcastle United. Thankfully, that afternoon found young Albert in Sheffield playing for Wednesday's reserves.

But there was one other tragedy, one that would affect Albert more than any of the other tear-jerking trio, as he succumbed to that dreaded illness dementia and was to spend his later days in the Riverside Care Home in Hyde, completely unaware of his surroundings or indeed, who he was or what he had achieved as a professional footballer, who at one time was the most expensive player in the British game.

Dementia was an opponent that no footballer, never mind the skilful Albert Quixall, could master. It is a heart-breaking illness, bringing suffering to both the individual and their family, coming at a time when those who knew nothing of the time of day, never mind the day of the week, should have been reminiscing with their grandchildren and great grandchildren about those days of old, when life was completely different.

For the likes of Albert Quixall, along with many who were his team mates, he should have been sitting at home with his international caps, medals and memories, recalling games and players from the past, from school pitches to Wembley. Days and events that were not simply forgotten, but were as if they never existed in the first place.

Born on August 9th 1933 to Albert and Doris [née Crossley], he was the second oldest of five children. Brother Roy was born the previous year, sisters Maureen and Jean in 1935 and 1937 respectively and brother George in 1940.

As a youngster, he attended Meynell Road School, polishing his footballing ability, as did thousands of others in the school playground, with local parks and streets also taking on the mantle of make-believe stadiums. He could be said to have taken some of his footballing ability from his father, as George could be found playing for Neepsend Ward in the Sheffield Unemployed League 'A' Division in the mid-1930's, whilst also helping his side to the Braithwaite Cup in April 1934.

Progressing to Meynell Road secondary school, Albert Quixall's ability with a ball at his feet pushed him to the forefront of the schoolboy game and it was a steady progression from the school team to Sheffield Boys and the biggest stepping stone of all, into the England Schoolboys side.

Although small in stature, he was selected as a thirteen-year-old to represent the Hillsborough area in the Sheffield Boys trial at Concord Park in mid-September 1946. Even at such an early age, and having just stepped out of primary school, his attributes were already noted, with a mention of the trial in the *Sheffield Star* sports edition the *"Green 'Un"* saying: *"Quixall who plays cricket for Sheffield Boys is an inside right, his ball control and passing were the feature of the trial."* Needless to say, he was selected for that Sheffield Boys side to face Nottingham Boys and, from the brief match report of the October 5th fixture, came: *"The brilliance of Quixall, the Meynell Road inside right, was the feature of the game,"* when he scored in his team's 5-3 defeat.

Three weeks later, on October 26th, he was again in the Sheffield Schools line-up, facing Selby in the English Schools Shield competition, and again finding his name prominent in the match reports. Right from the offset, he was involved in the action and was unlucky not to open the scoring, being denied by the post. He was, however, to score later in the game as the Sheffield Boys demolished their opponents 10-0.

Pressing the 'fast-forward' button to the fifties and sixties, Albert Quixall became a star attraction within the game and he was often worth the admission money alone; however, such a scenario wasn't unknown back in those immediate post-war years of the 1940's when he was nothing more than a mere schoolboy. In the lead up to a Daily Dispatch Trophy semi-final between Meynell Road and Southey Green on January 18th 1947, it could be considered that his name was used as a form of publicity: *"Southey have dominated schools football for three seasons, while Meynell Road have the present Sheffield right wing, Quixall, and Wright. This match will be worth going a long way to see."*

Sheffield Schoolboys Team. Back Row: Champion (Shirecliffe), Rixham (Owler Lane East), Scott (Owler Lane West), Stokes (Whitby Rd.), Skelton (Walkley). Front Row: Wright (Meynell Rd.), Quixall (Meynell Rd.), Browse (Wybourn), Dawson (Wincobank), Samwell (Philadelphia), Faries (Pipworth Rd.).

A week prior to that 'must see' encounter, Albert had captured the headlines, yet again, for his performance for Sheffield Boys against Derby Boys at Bramall Lane. *"The Skill Of Quixall"* shouted the headline, followed by: *"Quixall, the diminutive inside right, shone in the forward line, working and distributing the ball with a skill no professional could have outdone."*

Success and failure were all part and parcel of the schoolboy game and there was disappointment at St James' Park, following a defeat at the hands of Newcastle Boys in May 1947, and again by Liverpool Boys on home soil, despite the effervescent inside forward flitting between attack and defence during the 2-0 reversal.

The headlines and plaudits were not, however, exclusive to Albert's footballing ability as the summer months saw the boots placed to one side and cricket become the focus of his sporting life. Even here, his enthusiasm bubbled over and he found selection within the Sheffield Boys side. Again, it was with mixed results, but Albert being Albert, he still managed to capture a few lines in any newspaper reports. One such report on a game against Barnsley Boys related: *"No-one seemed to get into top gear except Quixall of Meynell Road, a star footballer, as many Sheffielders have seen, and now a most attractive and agile cover-point, and the only Sheffield batsman to show any bright enterprise. Well done Quixall."*

Due to his age, Albert was able to continue in the Sheffield Boys side for the 1947-48 season, his selection being taken for granted, but it was again with mixed results. Missed chances by his team mates, as he created the opportunities, resulted in a 1-0 defeat by Don and Dearne Boys in mid-October 1947, but it was the Meynell Road youngster who showed the way at the end of the month against Nottingham Boys when he was considered *"the best player on the field"*. Perhaps scoring the winning goal in the 2-1 victory, thirteen minutes from time, with a stunning twenty-five-yard drive, did much to claim that accolade.

November 1947 brought the announcement that he was the only Sheffield representative to have been selected for a trial match at Leeds the following month with a view towards the first schools' representative fixture since the war, between Yorkshire and London at Bradford Park Avenue's ground on New Years Day. *"If Quixall can bring his forwards into the game with those adroit passes at which he is so skilled, there should be no question about his cap"* was the view of more than the local Sheffield press following his appearance for 'The Reds' versus 'The Greens'.

While his Sheffield Boys outings produced a mixture of results, often ploughing a lone furrow up and down the field in an attempt to cultivate a victory, his Yorkshire Boys selection would have brought a wide smile to his face, if not a goal, during the course of the ninety minutes, as the London Boys were soundly beaten 6-0.

But by now, Albert had forsaken his usual inside-forward position and stepped back to the half-back line, although it was to bring some unwarranted criticism following a match against Chesterfield: *"Quixall displayed once again all his recognised tricks but still has a minor fault, not yet eradicated; he plays too far behind his forwards."* Although the same article on the schoolboy football scene closed with: *"It is a great pity that our own Quixall has not been given the chance to show what he can do in an international trial. He would have shone with his undoubted skill, for all round there was an ability to control and distribute the ball."* His slight build and blond hair would contribute much to him standing out amongst team mates and opponents alike, but it was his ability with a ball at his feet that really made the difference.

For one reason or another Albert didn't feature in the aforementioned Yorkshire v London fixture, but instead was involved in a Sheffield Boys v Nottingham Boys encounter at Meadow Lane that same day, in what was a period when he could rarely stop for breath, as two days later he was facing Leicester Boys.

The fixtures were by now coming thick and fast, and, with January 1948 less than a fortnight old, he was in the Sheffield Schoolboys side to face their Grimsby equivalent in the Victoria Cup second leg fixture, where he continued to feature at right half in the 4-3 win. A game that pushed him closer to that England Schoolboy international cap, with his selection confirmed prior to the two sides meeting again at Blundell Park at the end of March.

Wednesday March 31st was undoubtedly the biggest game in Albert Quixall's footballing life to date. Played under a blistering sun at Stockport County's Edgeley Park, it was England versus The Rest, in what was the final international trial: ninety minutes that would determine which of those young hopefuls taking part would pull on the white shirt of their country against Wales on April 8th.

Watched by a crowd of around 20,000, with conditions simply too warm for fast, up-tempo football, the two sides did turn in an exciting ninety minutes of football, although 'England' proved superior to their opponents in their 3-0 victory, through goals from Brennan, playing on his local ground and Birkett of Newton-le-Willows, who claimed two.

The expectancy at such fixtures is that 'The Rest' are merely making up the numbers and that the selected team would be those who turned out under 'England' or whatever, but not every trial match has an Albert Quixall on show and: *"though smaller, The Rest showed some of the best ideas and little Albert Quixall, of Sheffield, delighted, with some tricky and constructive play."* Such was his performance that there was no way he could be left out of the side and he was duly named in the England eleven.

"There is a natural feeling of jubilation and pride at the selection of Albert Quixall to play inside right for his country against Wales next Saturday at Coventry. Such an honour has been richly deserved, for Albert has played consistently brilliant football for the City team for the past two years" appeared in the 'Schools Football' column of the *Green 'Un* on Saturday April 3rd 1948. *"His display in the England versus the Rest final trial left the selectors in no doubt as to his ability, despite his lack of inches - he is only 5ft. 1in."*

"What is more important is that he still wears the same size in hats, and his teachers, who knew him well, affirm that the further football honours which will undoubtedly come his way will in no way affect his modest and likeable character."

THE ENGLAND TEAM
Left to right, standing: A. Malcolm (*captain*), C. B. Nicholas, R. S. Barnard, K. A. Martin, M. Jones, N. V. Deeley. *Seated:* C. Birkett, A. Quixall, B. Brennan, R. Spencer, D. S. Green.

So, Saturday April 10th 1948 found the fourteen-year-old Albert wandering into the home dressing room at Highfield Road Coventry, along with his teammates to prepare for the 'Victory Shield' international match against Wales, for what was to be the first of two schoolboy international caps.

A look through the Welsh line-up fails to conjure up any names of significance, but a number of those sharing the dressing room with Albert, whilst nervously chattering away to ward off those pre-match nerves, would later lock horns with him as rivals in the hustle and bustle of League football.

At left-back was Mark Jones, who was to become a colossus in the heart of the Manchester United defence. The two wing halves, as they were in those days, Andy Malcolm and Norman Deeley, went on to play for West Ham United and Wolverhampton Wanderers respectively. While the forward line saw Newton-le-Willows youngster, Cliff Birkett, as Albert's partner on the right wing, another who was destined for Old Trafford and Manchester United.

In the lead up to the fixture, the *Coventry Evening Telegraph* previewed the match with pen pictures of the England Boys, with that of A. Quixall (inside right) reading: *"Another small player 5ft 1½ins. he is a really brilliant and talented footballer, with astonishing ball control, skill and distribution."*

The 25,199 crowd must have released more than a few butterflies in the stomach of the youngsters of both sides, but it was the English lads who enjoyed the best of the ninety minutes, winning 2-1.

For some unknown reason, the reporter from the *Coventry Evening Telegraph* who was covering the match, spoke of Quixall, as the "Staffordshire" inside right, but the observer was correct in his assessment of the young number eight as being prominent in the early stages with some clever passing to both wings. An error in print of course, but at least he was making an impression. The Monday edition of the same newspaper, looking back at the match was to add, in reference to Albert – *"Here surely is another Mortensen in the making."* In the *Green 'Un* report, it mentioned: *"Sheffield's Quixall cleverly initiated several dangerous English attacks"*.

But somewhat strangely, the selectors were on something of a different wavelength to the man from the *Coventry Evening Telegraph*, as immediately following the victory over Wales, they selected the team to face Scotland at Aberdeen's Pittodrie's ground a fortnight later, omitting Albert and Deeley. A sub-heading proclaiming: *'Two Smallest Boys Dropped.'* Small they were, but compared to Norman Deeley, Albert was a giant, as the Staffordshire boy was a mere 4ft 10in, looking more like the team mascot in the pre-match team group photograph.

So, a fortnight later, on Saturday April 24th 1948, Albert should really have been playing schoolboy football in his native Sheffield, but due to an injury to centre-forward Brennan, he was drafted back into the England side, and along with his team mates made the long journey north to Aberdeen for what would have been nothing short of an adventure for those youngsters. It was, however, to be a long journey back south, as the boisterous home dressing room celebrated a single-goal victory. If it was of any consolation, the reporter from the *Sunday Post* considered Albert, along with Jones and Hart to have *"served the visitors well"*, while the local *Aberdeen Press and Journal* spoke of the substitute as being: *"Clever on the ball, putting some good passes away to his winger."* The *Aberdeen Press and Journal* man at the match was equally impressed, writing that although Scotland's Wylie *"was the best of the bunch, he was not so good as England's box of tricks – little Albert Quixall."*

No matter what level of the schoolboy game he participated in, he stood out, even the current England Schools Shield holders – Salford Boys, couldn't hold him as he was once again spoken of as being outstanding in Sheffield's 4-1 victory at Hillsborough on May 1st.

With schoolboy football now being something of the past, as was his education in general, there was no shortage of clubs vying for the signature of the teenager considered "the most promising young footballer in Sheffield," but there was only ever going to be one winner and that was Sheffield Wednesday, the team supported by both his father, a green keeper at Firth Park, and his grandfather.

Had their interest in football ranged between minimal to non-existent, and their allegiance being cemented elsewhere, then there is every possibility that Albert Quixall could have been a Notts County player. Playing in the annual Nottingham v Sheffield Cottee Cup fixture, the then twelve-year-old was spotted by ex-County president Mr. George Cottee and at the end of the ninety-minutes he was asked if he would like to join Notts County upon leaving school. The forthcoming reply was brief, yet polite, saying that he had promised his father that when the time came, he would sign for Wednesday.

Signing as an amateur, he was guaranteed football every week, as the Wednesday had decided to run a fourth team for the 1948-49 season, using a ground near to the Owlerton stadium. Although it was his local club, Sheffield Wednesday was the ideal location for the promising footballer, as unlike the vast majority of other clubs, they did not employ youngsters on their ground staff – not a pathway that the boys taken on by Sheffield Wednesday followed.

Wednesday's secretary-manager at the time when Albert fell into the 'apprentice' category was to say: "Any boys in whom we may be interested in are told to apply themselves to a trade, and even when they reach the age of 17, we do not encourage them to sign professional forms.

"Football is an uncertain profession, and we prefer youngsters to learn a trade or have a job which is not a blind alley occupation like professional football can be. Quixall, for example, is an apprentice-joiner."

As 1949 blended into 1950, Albert got a glimpse of what top class football was all about. He had obviously watched the Wednesday first team from time to time when not playing, but on Saturday January 7th 1950, along with five of his junior team mates, he accompanied the 'big boys' as they headed to Highbury to face Arsenal in an FA Cup third round tie.

Arsenal's single goal victory gave the youngsters little to cheer about, but the overall performance of the Wednesday team showed them the level that they had to aspire to, with the Gunners' manager, Tom Whittaker, making his way into the away dressing at full time, praising the Wednesday performance, whilst adding that he was looking forward to seeing them at Highbury again the following season as a First Division club.

Yes, the Sheffield Wednesday that Albert Quixall had joined were indeed a Second Division side, something else that spurred him on, wanting to play his part in seeing the team he supported back in the top flight, and on a permanent basis.

Promotion to the First Division was achieved at the end of that 1949-50 season, as runners-up to Tottenham Hotspur, but they were some nine points adrift, with sixteen drawn games to Tottenham's seven being the telling factor.

Albert Quixall's football education continued, not just with Sheffield Wednesday, but in representative football, playing for Sheffield and Hallamshire, helping them to success in the County Minor Championship final against Barnsley in a thrilling 6-4 encounter, scoring once.

This victory came a matter of days after a Wednesday 'A' team match against Brodsworth M.C. in the Yorkshire League; those who were a little out of sync with the football, outwith the Wednesday first team, and who read the *Sheffield Daily Telegraph* were brought slap bang up to date with Albert's progress: "Quixall Maturing On The Right Lines" were the headlines above a rather brief report.

Maturing he certainly was and he was rewarded with a professional contract at the end of the 1949-50 season, but despite the elevation to the ranks, he was still down the pecking order, remaining a member of the Wednesday 'A' team, playing against the likes of Ossett Town. You did have to learn to walk before you could run!

Albert was a quick learner. The 1950-51 season was barely out of the traps, when the likes of Ossett Town and the Yorkshire League were pushed aside for the Central League and the reserve sides of numerous senior clubs. If he could have chosen his opponents for his debut in the Wednesday second string, then local rivals Sheffield United would have been high on his list.

And so it was, on the afternoon of September 9th 1950, that he lined up in his familiar inside-right spot to face Sheffield United reserves at Bramall Lane and he took less than five minutes to make his mark on the game. A long pass out to Marriott on the Wednesday left saw the winger quickly return the ball into the centre, where Fletcher bundled the ball home.

"*In ball distribution, Quixall is a natural,*" the *Green 'Un* reporter had scribbled in his notebook before the referee's whistle signalled half time, when the teams were on level pegging at 1-1. In the second half there were no eye-catching moments from Quixall. Wednesday went behind again, and it was only a penalty three minutes from time that earned Wednesday a share of the points.

The match summary in the *Sheffield Daily Telegraph* the Monday following the game was equally praising: *"Quixall retains his uncanny knack of finding the unmarked man, and although wisely avoided the 'battle areas' shirked neither tackle nor challenge."*

Those comments were echoed in the same newspaper the following day in a report of the Wednesday Reserves 3-0 victory over Stoke City the previous night. *"Though there may be doubts about Quixall's physique, there can be none about his ability.*

"The certainly and accuracy of his passing, and his use of the open spaces, rate Quixall as Wednesday's best prospect."

Football, in what was those immediate post-war years, hadn't changed overly much as clubs continued to overcome the loss of players, grounds due to German bombing, as was the case of Manchester United, not to mention the lack of finance, with those once healthy bank balances decimated like streets of houses that had borne the brunt of those same German bombers. Although the modern-day game would see the sport become a business, with supporters being replaced by spectators/customers, clubs back in the early fifties were a business of sorts, many resembling the work-house from the not-too-distant past, employing boys barely out of short trousers as 'apprentice professionals.' Yes, those boys were in the main, talented footballers, they wouldn't be with a club otherwise, but they were also being used as what some considered to be 'slave-labour,' employed to carry out the menial tasks of cleaning boots, sweeping the terraces or painting the stands. "It's all part of the learning curve" came the reply, and to be fair, those same youngsters were more often than not, found apprenticeships with local joiners, builders or whatever, ensuring they had a trade to follow if a career in football was not to materialise. Some were perhaps more fortunate and were employed in the club offices. In Albert's case, however, he was an apprentice joiner.

Decades ago, reserve team football was awash with seasoned professionals unable to grasp that first team place due to form, injury or whatever, making it that learning curve for the likes of Albert Quixall and fellow youngsters like Derek Dooley. One fixture featuring the duo, against Liverpool on November 4th 1950, was certainly an education in the rougher side of the game, with Albert reportedly receiving 'severe buffetings,' but he stood up well to the physical abuse, scoring once in the 3-2 victory.

Those 'severe buffetings' were part and parcel of any aspiring professional's football education, and slowly Albert became accustomed to the often-brutal tactics employed against him, whilst adding some five inches to his height and overall physique.

But for every step forward, there would be one back, as it came as something of shock to Albert and his growing body of admirers, who had hoped for continual selection for the Central League side, that he was to find himself named amongst those on third team duty at Dinnington in the Yorkshire League: a competition he thought he had left far behind.

If he was annoyed, despondent, concerned or whatever, by his sudden demotion when everything appeared to be on track, he was left in total shock on Friday January 26th 1951, two weeks after that third team outing. Scanning the third team line-up for the following afternoon's fixture against Beighton, he found no mention of his name. Neither was he down to play against Everton in the Central League.

Any thoughts of sitting in the stand watching his team mates, or an afternoon's shopping, were quickly dispelled, as a glance at the first team sheet saw his name in the inside-right position to face Leicester City at Filbert Street.

Yes, it was only a friendly, both teams having made an early exit from the FA Cup at the first hurdle, but it was first team football: what Albert had craved since signing on the dotted line for Sheffield Wednesday.

The ninety minutes were far from memorable, perhaps due to there being little at stake, with the result being all but meaningless, but for Albert it was the big stage, an opportunity to prove to his manager that he was ready for that step up into the First Division cauldron on a regular basis.

The *Green 'Un*, a Saturday night 'must read' within the locality, summarised the game as being: *"not a great one, though there were several players who did well, and among them none was better than Quixall, who played through the game with steadiness and at times showed an ability to seize openings."*

An early Leicester goal turned out to be the only one of the ninety minutes, but minutes prior to that solitary goal, the young seventeen-year-old debutant had almost given Wednesday the lead with a rising drive that flew narrowly over the bar.

Having got his foot in the first team door, Albert was going to do his upmost to keep it wedged open. He had, however, to keep his expectations harnessed for the time being, as seven days later he was back on Central League duty at Newcastle, partnering Alan Finney on the right flank. As always, he was heavily involved throughout the ninety minutes, playing his part in the 3-1 victory.

February 10th was, again, FA Cup day, so instead of filling the void with a somewhat meaningless friendly, Sheffield Wednesday locked horns with neighbours United in a County Cup semi-final. Treating the ninety minutes as though he was only one step away from an appearance under the Wembley twin towers, those in attendance could only have been impressed by Albert: *"Young Quixall further confirmed the promise he has shown of developing into a first-class inside forward, with almost perfect ball control, and intelligent distribution"*, the good old *Green 'Un* told its readers who hadn't bothered to attend and see for themselves the boy whose name was now on everyone's lips.

Despite that commendable performance, there was still no first team re-call a week later, which was perhaps a blessing in disguise.

On the afternoon of February 17th, Albert was in action at Hillsborough for the Wednesday second string against West Bromwich Albion. Twenty-five minutes into the game, he scored the opening goal from a free-kick as the Albion defence hesitated, expecting the kick to be in their favour. Across the ninety minutes, he once again demonstrated his all-round ability and showed that he and his front-line partner Alan Finney had adopted a fine understanding.

Back in the dressing room, buoyant with yet another positive result, not to mention performance, he was suddenly hit with devastating news. His grandfather, George Quixall, had collapsed and died at Newcastle whilst watching the Wednesday first team at St James Park.

What had resulted in a 2-0 reversal on Tyneside, left Wednesday anchored at the foot of the First D

ivision, a point behind Aston Villa and two behind third and fourth bottom Huddersfield Town and Chelsea. With the business end of the season fast approaching, the Wednesday management team had to do something, and quickly, if relegation was to be avoided, more so with a ninety-minute encounter with fellow strugglers Chelsea next up on the fixture list on February 24th 1951.

With the still wet behind the ears pairing of Quixall and Finney having shown up well in the Central League, it was decided that there was nothing to be lost by throwing the seventeen-year-olds into the First Division fray and the pair were given their first team debuts for the crucial Hillsborough encounter.

Albert, and Alan Finney, although not inseparable, were to become good friends and were known around Hillsborough as 'Null and Void', although no-one knew why, or who even thought up the names. Albert's own nickname of 'Snuffy' was easier to determine, as it was down to his habitual sniff!

Of the pair, it was Albert Quixall who shone through the darkening clouds around Sheffield, showing some fine touches, never afraid to take on his man and was unfortunate not to find his name on the scoresheet.

A goal down at half time, Wednesday drew level through Hughes, then on the hour mark they were in front. Judging the ball perfectly as it headed his way, Albert was onto it in a flash, made a few yards before shooting for goal. Chelsea centre-half Harris made a brave attempt to keep the ball out, but inadvertently could only help it over the line. As much as he would like to have claimed the goal, it was the Chelsea man who had sent it over the line. Some newspapers, however, did credit the goal to Albert.

He might also have won his side a penalty when shoved over in the area, a spot kick that may well have given Wednesday both points instead of just the one from a 2-2 draw.

In his match summary, Fred Walters of the Green 'Un wrote: *"There does not appear to be any reason why Wednesday should be afraid to play Quixall. In mid-field he had as much craft as the next player, and moreover, there were times when he showed unmistakably that he is a quick thinker.*

"Moreover, there is little need for the club to worry about him keeping out of danger. He plays with his head, and when a player does that, he has generally a good idea of what to expect."

The People correspondent was to write: *"Best feature of the Wednesday scene was the success of seventeen-years-old Albert Quixall, former Sheffield boy international. He scored a brilliant goal in his League debut, cleverly tricking Hughes and then drawing Medhurst from his goal."*

So, that long-awaited, perhaps overdue, debut had come and gone, but there was to be little breathing space between that first and second game, as, a mere two days after facing Chelsea, Manchester United were crossing the Pennines into the White Rose County.

There was no repeat performance from the youngsters, or Wednesday for that matter, as United scored four without reply.

"The players were completely without confidence – except for the two newest members the side, two 17-year-old forwards, Quixall, inside right from Sheffield, and Finney, from the Doncaster district.

"In a year or two these may be exceptionally able footballers. Their talent was plain to see, particularly because so many their teammates were out of form, but just now they are in danger of tiring themselves out for lack of a cool head to direct their energy and abundant skill.

It was difficult to recognise the others as the same men who stormed Wednesday into such a strong position in the Second Division last season."

Somewhat surprisingly, it was another fledgling youngster who controlled the game and received the plaudits – eighteen-year-old Mark Jones, himself a Yorkshire lad and a former England Schools teammate of Albert's, with United casually brushing aside the forlorn Wednesday eleven with goals from Pearson, Downie, Rowley and McShane, leaving Wednesday cemented at the bottom of the First Division table on twenty points, the same number as fellow strugglers Aston Villa, but having played two games more. Huddersfield were on twenty-one, Chelsea on twenty-two. The clock was ticking.

But despite what could be regarded as 'instant success' in the hustle and bustle of the First Division, where young, somewhat naive players, could be eaten for breakfast, Quixall, and Finney, were both left out of Wednesday's next game against Wolverhampton Wanderers. "Rested" was the word used by the Hillsborough management.

Whether the youngsters would have made any difference is debatable, as Wolves, like Manchester United before them, scored four without reply. At Liverpool a fortnight later, although the goals against were reduced by two, Wednesday still lost by the odd goal in three. Second Division football at Hillsborough next season was now more a probability than a possibility.

If the thought of relegation had infiltrated the mind of Albert Quixall, he was given more to think about with Wednesday's signing of Jackie Sewell from Notts County, a £30,000 or £35,000 world record signing, depending on whatever newspaper you read. Here was another player, an experienced one at that, to compete against for a first team place. With the new-boy scoring on his debut against Liverpool, the darkening cloud above Albert's head must have grown larger, but it was no match-winning goal as Wednesday stumbled to yet another defeat – it had now been five games without a victory, with relegation becoming more of a reality with each passing day.

Albert's 'rest' period turned into something more akin to a holiday, as he was not to use a peg on the dressing room wall on a first team match-day for the remainder of that 1950-51 season, his two appearances, against Chelsea and Manchester United, being the sum total for the campaign. It is difficult to say if his exclusion from the first-team was justified, as record signing Sewell only found the net another five times in the remaining nine fixtures, but only two of those were lost, with Woodhead, Froggatt and Rickett taking up the fight in an effort to avoid relegation.

The relegation battle was arguably the reason behind Albert's exclusion, his teenage years going against him, his enthusiasm and undoubted talent being of little consideration as the Wednesday management relied more on experience to claw out the much sought after points.

Despite that end of season run with only three defeats in the final ten games, Sheffield Wednesday were relegated to the Second Division, despite finishing on the same number of points as Chelsea – thirty-two. The eighty-three goals they had conceded, compared with the Londoners sixty-five proving their downfall. Everton had also finished the season on thirty-two points, and it was their meagre forty-eight goals scored was to prove their downfall. Somewhat ironically, Wednesday hit them for six, without reply, on the final day of the season.

If there was compensation for the lack of first team outings, although nothing could replicate the thrill of running out in front of a packed ground, reaping the acclaim of the hordes on the terracing, it came in the form of a Sheffield County Cup winners medal following a 2-1 victory over Doncaster Rovers on May 12th, in what was a physically intimidating ninety minutes.

Although it was Second Division fare on the menu for Sheffield Wednesday and Albert Quixall for the 1951-52 season, there may well have been flickers of doubt as to where that season would take him in his journey towards firmly establishing himself in the world of professional football, more so when Jackie Sewell, his nemeses, had notched some thirty-one goals on an FA tour of Australia and Tasmania. Below average opposition perhaps, but...

The 1951-52 season kicked off on Saturday August 18th, with the nineteen-year-old Albert Quixall boarding the Wednesday team coach and heading off to Lancashire and Deepdale, Preston, to face North End's second string in the opening Central League fixture of the season. He would rather have been sitting in the Hillsborough dressing room, preparing to face Doncaster Rovers, but if it wasn't to be, then he simply had to grin and bear it and hope that it would not be too long before that first team opportunity once again came his way.

With Preston inflicting a 3-0 defeat, it was a long journey back, the first team's 3-1 victory over Doncaster bringing little in the way of sunshine on a dismal afternoon and, despite something of an indifferent start, the victory over Doncaster being followed by a 3-1 defeat at Leicester City and a 3-3 draw at Everton, two home fixtures, against Leicester City and Southampton did produce victories, 1-0 and 3-1 respectively. Added to the disappointment of no first team football was the fact that Jackie Sewell had scored five goals in the opening five fixtures.

Despite the two favourable results against Leicester and Southampton, the name Quixall had appeared on the squad list that was pinned up on the notice board for the third home fixture in a row, against Birmingham City on Monday September 3rd. There was, however, no place in the starting line-up and if that was disappointing, then there was more to follow five days later when he received an ankle injury playing for the reserves against Derby County at Owlerton.

The injury was nothing serious and it certainly did not prevent him from being selected for the Central League XI to face last season's champions Wolverhampton Wanderers at Molineux on September 29th, but being selected was to be the only honour, as the current champions ran out 3-1 winners.

Having been relegated at the end of the 1950-51 season, Wednesday were determined to regain First Division status as quickly as possible and the start to that 1951-52 campaign had been favourable in their hopes that it could be achieved at the first time of asking. However, with three victories, two draws and a defeat in the opening half dozen fixtures, a 1-1 draw against Birmingham City nudging them into second spot, the road suddenly changed from being long and straight to a series of hair-pin bends and Wednesday, unable to control the momentum, veered completely off course and by the end of September, they had crashed to seventeenth.

Quixall's joinery apprenticeship would give him something to fall back on if the cruel hands of fate prevented him from making the grade within the game and perhaps also something to adapt to when those legs were no longer capable of enduring ninety minutes of football. Young master Quixall also served his footballing apprenticeship under the watchful eye of another skilled craftsman, lining up in the Wednesday reserve side alongside a certain Derek Dooley, not mention his nemesis in more experienced Jackie Sewell.

Although Albert was still to mature, find his niche within the game, Sheffield-born Dooley was an out-and-out goal scorer. He had somehow escaped the clutches of Wednesday, and neighbours United for that matter, and signed for Lincoln City as an amateur. He became a free-scoring frontman who, despite being only seventeen, had enjoyed a couple of run-outs in the Lincoln reserve side during the 1946-47 season. Local newspaper match reports frequently used the words "Dooley scored," as he headed the Lincoln reserves scoring charts for two seasons.

Despite the goals, Dooley had eyes on one of his home town clubs and, in June 1947, he joined Wednesday, simply giving his reason as he did "not intend to play with the home crowd against him."

Once installed at Hillsborough, he was to score fifty-five goals in thirty-eight third team Yorkshire League appearances (eight in one game), and thirty-seven in forty-nine Central League outings over the course of three seasons.

Like Quixall, his game time in the relegation-haunted season of 1950-51 was limited, a solitary ninety minutes was all he could register, but due to the indifferent Wednesday form in the early weeks of the 1951-52 season, something had to be done if a prolonged stay in the second tier of the English game was not to be endured. So, having lost three in a row: 3-2 at Leeds United,

5-3 at Rotherham United and 2-1 at Cardiff City, something had to give, and manager, Eric Taylor, turned to twenty-year-old Dooley, who had netted thirteen goals already with the reserves, seventeen-year-old Alan Finney and eighteen-year-old Albert to face Barnsley at Hillsborough on October 6th.

Dooley took the plaudits with both goals in the 2-1 victory, then having two blank weekends, really went to town with one in a 2-2 draw with Queens Park Rangers, five in a 6-0 thrashing of Notts County, followed by four doubles and a hat-trick, another single and a four, in the next nine fixtures.

Perhaps overshadowed by his Central League colleague, the reporter from the *Yorkshire Post and Leeds Intelligencer* (I kid you not) wrote following the 1-0 victory over Hull City on October 13th, where Alan Finney claimed the headlines: *"Wednesday, however, had the finished footballer – a miniature Sewell in little Quixall, who showed rare talents for one of his age."*

This was perhaps the turning point of Albert Quixall's career. He had been presented with that first team opportunity, arguably at the cost of points to his club in their League ambitions when selecting more senior and experienced players may have produced better results. But his boyish enthusiasm carried him through, avoiding the wrath of the man on the terrace, and, without being selfish, he was more than grateful to once again be sampling first team football.

As the leaves on the trees turned to a golden brown and October edged into November, the well-greased Wednesday rollercoaster rattled along. A 5-3 reversal at Luton Town on November 10th proved to be nothing more than a minor irritation, as normality was restored seven days later with the 2-1 win against Bury kick-starting an unbeaten run of seven games.

November had in turn given way to December, and Christmas was little more than seventeen days away; the paper chains, tinsel and the decorated trees had still to make an appearance, but dear old Father Christmas turned up early – Albert Quixall had been noticed by the old guy in red and white, who despatched a special present his way, in the form of that first League goal, against West Ham United at Upton Park on Saturday December 8th.

The Hammers were no match for the effervescent Wednesday youngsters and were four down by the half-time whistle and six behind at the end of the ninety minutes.

Forget Dooley's hat-trick, never mind his nineteen in ten games, or for that matter Redfern Froggatt's double, it was only Wednesday's fifth goal that mattered. The thump of leather against leather, the spherical object passing the goalkeeper's fingers, the bulging net behind him, the inner jubilation and the acclaim of the crowd. The duck was broken.

In reality, it was nothing spectacular, indeed you will do well to find a mention of it other than being a "snap goal" or: "Quixall completed the scoring towards the end".

The wait to get his name on the scoresheet had not been as prolonged as it seemed: the gap between that initial first team appearance and that first goal, when judged against minutes played, was actually minimal. The gap between the first and the second, however, would be much longer.

In the 'resting' of Jackie Sewell, Albert was seen as his obvious replacement, but the big money signing was to return to the fray for the 4-0 victory over Everton, fellow relegation side of a few months previous, with Albert the player to step aside. That 4-0 victory was to shove Wednesday into top spot in the Second Division for the first time that season.

It was obviously a huge disappointment to Albert. It was not as if he had been playing badly or not contributing to the team in any way, it was arguably down to nothing more than a "we have paid a lot of money for a player, so we have to play him" outlook. Sewell had, to be honest, made a telling contribution to the Wednesday side, his five goals in the opening four fixtures testimony to that, but, with the current form of Derek Dooley, it could be debated that his purchase, at what was an eye-watering price, was somewhat unnecessary.

The Christmas period would have seen Albert rather despondent, a festive season that could have been better, but, like Christmas itself, that disappointment was over in a flash, as he was back in the Wednesday starting line-up on December 29th against Southampton, when Sewell was apparently injured, keeping his place for the local derby against neighbours United on January 5th.

With Sewell having recovered from his thigh injury, he was back in the starting line-up to face Bradford Park Avenue in the FA Cup, with Albert again stepping down, a move that did not go down well in some quarters, more so following the 2-1 defeat. Being able to concentrate solely on the League was at least some form of minor compensation.

A reoccurrence of Sewell's thigh injury in the cup tie yet again opened the door for Albert and he was back in the first team to face Leeds United on January 19th, but his presence did little to help Wednesday as they suffered their third defeat in a row; a 3-3 draw at Rotherham a week later making it four games without a win.

With 1952 getting into its stride, the career of Albert Quixall looked at last to have turned a corner. With Jackie Sewell having recovered again from injury, it wasn't Albert who stood down to allow the big-money man back into the side, but Alan Finney. Although disappointed that his friend had been omitted, Albert was more than grateful not to have been dropped yet again.

Despite that trio of games without a victory, the 4-2 victory at home to Cardiff City on February 9th catapulted Wednesday back to the top of the Second Division, with the business end of the season slowly approaching.

Having bounced between the top eight positions in the Second Division over the past couple of months, there were smiles all around Hillsborough when Sheffield Wednesday returned to the top of the pile following that 4-2 victory over the Welsh side, but those smiles were soon turned upside down following what the press would term as a "nine-goal thriller", but, as far as Wednesday were concerned, a 5-4 defeat at the hands of Yorkshire neighbours Barnsley.

The March winds blew in two victories: a 6-0 walk-over against Hull City and 2-1 over Queens Park Rangers, but that turned out to be nothing more than a slight breeze, with two draws: 0-0 draw at Blackburn and 2-2 against Notts County failing to see that coveted top spot reclaimed. It simply kept the championship and that second promotion place up for grabs, as a mere four points were all that separated the top seven clubs. Birmingham City and Nottingham Forest sat on forty-two, Wednesday one behind, with Leicester City another point behind, all having played thirty-five games. Next came Cardiff City and Leeds United, both on thirty-nine points, but having played only thirty-four games, while Rotherham United had thirty-eight from their thirty-five games and Sheffield United were on thirty-seven from their thirty-five.

With a blank Saturday on the fixture list, due to that early FA Cup exist, Albert found himself in the Central League side against Bury, scoring in the 2-0 victory on March 8th, but he was return to what was slowly becoming an all-star Wednesday front line of Finney or Froggatt, Sewell, Dooley, Quixall and Whitaker, but as the results have shown, that 6-0 goal-fest against Hull City, whilst not producing a drought, failed to ignite the blue touchpaper.

The final month of the season promised to be a busy one for Albert and his team mates, with seven fixtures cramped into a twenty-four-day period, those crucial few weeks kicking off with the visit of Luton Town to Hillsborough.

Twenty-four hours prior to the April 2nd fixture, the *Bedfordshire and Hertfordshire Pictorial* in its preview of the game, carried pen-pictures of the Wednesday players; *"The youngest player in the side. Albert Quixall is only 18, but has a surprisingly mature football brain. At Sheffield they are certain that he is a future English international and he already knows what it's like to play for an England XI as he has played for his country as a schoolboy. Is rather frail as the moment, but is worth his place in the side as he is a fine tactician, despite his tender years."*

Although he failed to score, and as much as he would liked to have captured the headlines to convince the readers of that newspaper that its writer was not simply being polite, centre stage was captured, and not for the first time, by Derek Dooley, who not only scored two in the 4-0 victory, but broke the Wednesday goalscoring record, previously held by Jimmy Trotter with thirty-seven League and two FA Cup goals. Dooley had now claimed thirty-nine League and one FA Cup goal in only twenty-five appearances. Those two goals, plus the contribution from Rickett and Sewell, took Wednesday back to the top of the table. One down, six to go, the race had entered its final straight.

Three days following that emphatic 4-0 victory over Luton, Wednesday headed into Lancashire to face Bury, and it turned into something of a dour encounter with the visitors failing to find anything resembling their best form. "Taffy" Williams in the *Green 'Un* was of the opinion that their forward movements *"were too close to create many openings,"* but was quick to heap praise on Albert *"who stood out for his ball control and distribution,"* not to mention his goal.

Playing conditions were not the best, with the pitch greasy underfoot and neither side being able to settle into any form of rhythm. A low centre from Rickett should have resulted in the opening goal, but the usually competent Dooley completely missed the ball and, having rolled on to Froggatt, the equally capable goal scorer shot wide. But it wasn't all Wednesday in those opening exchanges, as Bury could also have taken an early lead, but Greenhalgh's rising drive was tipped over the bar by McIntosh in the visitor's goal.

With twenty-eight minutes gone, the deadlock was finally broken. Froggatt sent Sewell scurrying down the wing and having briefly controlled the ball, sent a low cross into the Bury penalty area where Albert seized the opportunity and scored with a low shot from six yards out.

Bury quickly regained their grip of the game and McIntosh was again called upon to make notable saves, a low drive from Cameron and a header from Bodie, but they were soon on the back foot once again and were to find themselves further behind five minutes before the break when Albert's centre found the head of Dooley and it was 2-0.

Resting momentarily on their laurels, Wednesday were caught out within a minute when Plant pulled a goal back and the home side continued to press as the second half got underway.

Despite the pressure heaped upon Wednesday, to not only make an instant return to the top flight, but to do so as champions, it was Albert Quixall who stood out at Gigg Lane that afternoon. Perhaps his youthful enthusiasm carried him along regardless of anything else, but there was no doubting that here was a player whose footballing ability was way beyond the age that his birth certificate confirmed.

His performance over the course of that ninety minutes, however, would not have earned him the maximum ten out of ten, as he should have claimed a second, early in that second half, as with only Goram to beat, he slipped the ball past the post, but anything less than 9.5 would have been an injustice.

Easter was arguably the telling point of the season: three games over a four-day period that would determine promotion and relegation issues. For Wednesday, an away fixture at Brentford on Good Friday was coupled with the visit of Swansea City to Hillsborough twenty-four hours later and the return fixture with Brentford on Easter Monday.

How many of the thirty-six thousand who packed into Brentford's ground that Good Friday afternoon had come to see Albert Quixall is debatable, but by the end of the afternoon, if they had previously been unaware of his capabilities, his name was on their lips just as much as Derek Dooley's hat-trick, his forty-fourth goal for the season, in Wednesday's 3-2 victory.

Ten minutes into the game, Wednesday were in front. A needlessly conceded corner was headed on by Albert, not the biggest player on the pitch by any manner of means, Sewell continuing the forward momentum, that ended with Dooley heading home.

Four minutes later it was 2-0. A Gannon free kick once again saw Albert rise above the pack, but his acrobatic twisting header, which was worthy of a goal in itself, was blocked by Brentford keeper Newton, but failing to hold the ball, he could do nothing as Dooley stepped in to nudge the ball home.

It was a game in which Albert once again shone, outdoing his more senior on-field companions who included the notable Tommy Lawton.

Brentford pulled a goal back due to a slip by McIntosh who fumbled the ball into his own net following a cross from Bragg, but Dooley was soon back on the score sheet, netting his third following a cross from Sewell. It was just as well, as McIntosh again was at fault, failing to connect when attempting to punch clear, allowing Dare to simply walk the ball into the vacant goal.

Lawton thought he had snatched an equaliser, but the referee decided that there had been an infringement in the Wednesday goal mouth and disallowed it.

Some might have been of the opinion that if there was a flaw to Albert Quixall's game then it was in his lack of goals, with his two for the season to date something of a meagre return. His overall contribution, however, could certainly not be ignored as recent results proved. No one grumbled or even commented on that lack of contribution to the goals-for column as they meandered away from Hillsborough at tea time on Saturday April 12th and, although there were certainly moans about the dropped point from the 1-1 draw with Swansea Town, it was Albert's goal that ensured a share of the points. It couldn't, however, prevent Wednesday from relinquishing top spot to Birmingham City.

Wednesday were denied an early penalty when Dooley went down as he was tackled inside to box. Then moments later, Albert dashed forward, veering in on goal, but as King in the Swansea goal left his line, the angle was now too tight and his effort crashed into the side netting.

A raised linesman's flag was to deny Swansea the opening goal and they had to wait until the seventieth minute before they could eventually claim the first strike of the afternoon through Beech, with McIntosh once again being found wanting and allowing the ball to curl over his head and into the net.

It looked as though it was going to be a costly mistake by the Wednesday keeper as they struggled to maintain any form of cohesion as the minutes ticked away. Indeed, many were of the opinion that they were about to witness their team's first defeat in eight games, and a vital one at that.

Four minutes remained; defeat looked inevitable as Wednesday pressed forward, more in hope than anything else. A centre from Froggatt had been headed goalwards by Sewell, but was beaten out by King. Possession was quickly regained and the ball found its way to Albert who, keeping his cool, beat King with a superb shot from the edge of the penalty area to rescue a point.

"*Sheffield Wednesday wonder boy, eighteen-year-old Albert Quixall, notched the equaliser in the last minute against Swansea to keep Wednesday in the running*" proclaimed *The People*. The *Green 'Un* headline said it all: "*Quixall saves Wednesday*" – "*A dramatic goal by Quixall in the closing minutes was a valuable one for Wednesday. Just when the crowd had taken it for granted that Swansea had the game won at Hillsborough, Quixall, with a glorious shot, saved the day.*"

Not a match-winning strike, but one that was lauded as such, as it kept Wednesday hot on the heels of Birmingham City, a point behind, with a two-point gap between them and third-placed Nottingham Forest. Four games remained. Nothing was written in stone.

If Albert's late strike against Swansea was pivotal in that race for the championship, the results of Easter Monday were equally so. Wednesday played host to Brentford and secured a 2-0 victory thanks to Sewell and an own goal, while Birmingham City were beaten 3-1 at Ninian Park, Cardiff, a defeat that saw Wednesday leapfrog into top spot, now a point ahead of their Midlands challengers and three in front of Forest who had dropped a point in a goalless encounter with Leeds United. Although nothing was certain, promotion now looked more than a possibility.

In the build up to the penultimate fixture of the season against Coventry City, 'Nemo' of the *Coventry Daily Telegraph*, debated the overall quality of Derek Dooley and mentioned, albeit in name only, Jackie Sewell. "*But I hope that the other inside forward, Quixall, will be in the side. This youngster – he is not yet 20 – is a clever, brainy type of player who should, with a little luck, go far in the game.*"

'Nemo' got his wish granted: how could Albert not be included in the Wednesday line-up? Nevertheless, he didn't waste much in the way of pencil lead on extolling the virtues of his performance, as Albert, and fellow inside man Jackie Sewell were subdued by Coventry's Dorman and Cook, but thankfully the Highfield Road side had no answer to Derek Dooley who grabbed both goals, taking his total to forty-six, a post-war record, in the 2-0 victory. It mattered little if Albert was for once subdued, as the two points ensured Wednesday, not just promotion, but the championship itself, making a welcome return to the First Division that they had vacated twelve months previously.

With time to reflect on the afternoon's ninety minutes 'Nemo' penned in the Monday edition of the *Coventry Evening Telegraph* "*As I anticipated, 18-years-old Quixall was more dangerous than costly Jackie Sewell.*"

The razzamatazz of the modern game when it comes to last day of the season trophy presentations is a far cry from that of the more sedate 1950's when there was no silverware in sight and nothing more than the sweat stained players making an impromptu appearance in the directors' box alongside chairman Mr. W. Ferniehough.

As for the previous ninety minutes, Wednesday were stunned as visitors West Ham United scored twice in a minute as half time beckoned. Thankfully two second half goals, from Froggatt and the ever-dependable Derek Dooley saved the Wednesday blushes and allowed them to finish two points ahead of Birmingham City.

The adulation from the throngs in front of the Hillsborough stand became more subdued, the players having departed to the more sedate sanctuary of the dressing room and finished their celebratory bottles of brown ale or whatever. Afterwards, it wasn't a case of Albert and his team mates heading home, throwing their boots into a cupboard and forgetting about them for a couple of months or so; the club had arranged a tour of Switzerland, where they would come face to face with the likes of the familiar Grasshoppers, Inter Milan, the totally unfamiliar St Gall, (against whom Albert scored twice in the 5-1 win), Bellinzona District, German side Fuerth and a Swiss Select. Would Blackpool and its Golden Mile have been more preferrable?

SHEFFIELD WEDNESDAY: SECOND DIVISION CHAMPIONS

Standing (left to right): A. W. Brown (trainer-coach), D. F. Witcomb, E. Gannon, K. Bannister, D. Dooley, C. Turton, N. W. Curtis, D. McIntosh. Seated: R. Froggatt, J. Sewell, E. Taylor (secretary-manager), A. Quixall, W. Rickett

CHAPTER TWO
THE ONLY WAY IS UP

So, Sheffield Wednesday were back in the First Division, where they had struggled in the not-too-distant past. In this division, the opposition were arguably more experienced, the defenders tougher and wiser, particularly when it came to facing relative youngsters like Albert Quixall. You didn't have as much time on the ball as you might have enjoyed in the Second Division, but it was all part of the learning curve and one that the Wednesday youngster had to endure if he was to continue what plaudits considered his pathway to greater things.

If Albert and his Wednesday teammates felt confident within themselves, and the First Division held no fears as the dawn of the 1952-53 season approached, then they were in for a rude awakening.

On the eve of the new season, Bob Ferrier of the *Daily Mirror*, whose grandfather played for Wednesday, paid a visit to Hillsborough: "*one of Britain's finest football grounds,*" where the expectations were of "*aiming for the top four,*" the *Mirror* correspondent himself being of the belief that Wednesday "*are better equipped for the First Division.*" It started well enough with a point at home in a 2-2 draw against last season's FA Cup winners, Newcastle United, on August 23rd, in front of over 55,000.

There was little or no rustiness as far as the play of Albert Quixall was concerned. He came out of the traps strongly, going close with a header, before seeing two long range shots blocked. Newcastle's legendary Jackie Milburn was to say: *"They have a future star in nineteen-year-old inside forward Albert Quixall. He is a bit on the small side but that doesn't matter, as Ernie Taylor has proved repeatedly. Albert has everything, and is more than good in the air for his size. Watch out for his name."*

An equally notable display against Liverpool at Anfield followed, where again only fine goalkeeping kept his name off the score sheet, but on this occasion, a last-minute goal from Baron denied Wednesday of another point. The *Liverpool Daily Post* reporter certainly didn't show any hint of bias when he penned: *"young Quixall stamped himself indelibly as an inside forward of England class,"* adding that: *"he was also the games outstanding forward."*

The outstanding forward he may well have been, but it soon became obvious, if it hadn't already been assumed, that Wednesday relied heavily on Derek Dooley's goals and with that reservoir of goals drying up like a river amid a long hot summer, the Hillsborough side would struggle.

That point on the opening day was satisfactory, while the single goal defeat at Anfield was down to little more than bad luck, but failing to gain anything from the two home fixtures against Liverpool and Charlton Athletic hammered home the point that Wednesday were perhaps not the First Division side they thought they were, and, having failed to score in four of those five opening fixtures, they were going to struggle throughout the season ahead if Dooley didn't deliver or someone else stepped up to the mark. The wearing of blue and white ankle socks for training purposes, instead of the heavier match day attire, proved to be of little benefit.

As in the second fixture of the season against Liverpool, luck was not on Wednesday's side when the two sides met again at Hillsborough on September 3rd, as McIntosh in the home goal was forced to vacate his goal for forty-five minutes due to a broken arm. Having been made well aware of Albert's capabilities at Anfield the previous week, he was well policed by the Merseysider's defence and seldom given time to cause any danger.

Four games played, a 4-0 defeat against Cardiff City tucked in between the two fixtures against Liverpool, with only two goals scored and nine conceded, called for action, so much so, that the Wednesday management took the bull by the horns and despite the lack of goals shocked everyone by dropping Derek Dooley for the visit of Charlton Athletic.

In the past, it could well have been Albert who was demoted to the Central League side, as goal droughts from star strikers were nothing uncommon, but for a centre-forward to score goals, the opportunities have to be crafted out, conjured up out of nowhere, and this was something that Albert Quixall was more than capable of doing. However, the Charlton match, a 3-0 defeat proved that Jordan, Dooley's replacement was nowhere near First Division material and that Albert, along with Sewell, missed Dooley's presence up front and therefore struggled through the tortuous ninety minutes.

Within a month of the campaign getting underway, Wednesday were propping up the table with a record of: played five, won none, drew one, lost four, with two goals for, both scored on the opening day, and twelve against.

Had the Charlton result been otherwise, then Derek Dooley might have endured a longer spell in the Wednesday second team, but two goals in the Central League fixture against Sheffield United proved that he had certainly not lost the knack of putting the ball in the back of the net, coupled with the inability of his replacement to show even a hint that he deserved a second run-out in the team, saw Dooley returned to the first team starting line-up to face Tottenham Hotspur at Hillsborough.

His return still saw that first goal of the season fail to materialise, but goals from Finney and Sewell kick-started Wednesday's season, with a clean sheet thrown in for good measure. The footballer-cum-miner Alan Finney took the man-of-the-match awards, but his name disappeared from the headlines within hours, replaced by that of his friend and team mate.

"*Young Blood For England*" screamed the *Daily Mirror* headlines on the morning of Tuesday September 16th 1952.

"*He is nineteen, just 5ft 5ins., with a shock of fair hair and a bright, attractive button face.*

"*He collects Frankie Laine and Nat "King" Cole records, goes dancing and plays table tennis and badminton at the local youth club. He is an apprentice joiner, a happy, personable teenager like thousands of others.*

"*But Albert Quixall is something more. He is also a great footballer, for Sheffield Wednesday. Albert took that as automatic – it couldn't be any other club.*

"*A very few years back, Albert, the local lad, stood starry-eyed on the soaring Hillsborough terraces, again as thousands of other boys do at all the great football grounds around our country.*

"*His only ambitions were to play for Wednesday, and maybe one day, for England, and the progressions seemed inevitable,*" wrote Bob Ferrier.

He continued: *"Now Albert wears the proud blue and white stripes and holds firmly to the inside left position in the Wednesday League side. Speed, rifle-accurate passing and a simplified, streamlined technique make him a great inside forward in the post-war Mortensen-Sewell fashion.*

"Already, the name of Quixall is apt to be bandied about when FA selectors cast their eyes around the sporting scene. Albert is clearly one for the book, but what I am concerned about is how the international future of Quixall, and a dozen others like him, is to be nursed.

"Albert Quixall is the living proof that England CAN stay on top internationally. He and others, like Bill Holden, George Hannah, Johnny Berry, Ray Barlow, Parry of Derby, Broadbent of Wolves, have convinced me that the stream of Soccer talent flows as strongly as has ever.

"This is not to claim that Quixall is ready for a place in the England team. He must get a few more games under his studs before that day comes.

"Yet in a game which would have been an ideal testing bench for some of these young players – that against the Irish League at Wolverhampton next week – the League selectors have insisted on playing what is the full international side."

As Ferrier wrote, time was indeed on Albert's side and his talent was obvious to all, but back in those draconian days of the 1950's, and for the early part of the 1960's, selection for the international side, not just in England, but over the border in Scotland as well, was one of the 'perks' of being classed as a selector, faceless individuals who had more than likely never kicked a ball in earnest. Their decisions were often baffling, never mind biased, to say the least.

The 2-0 victory over Tottenham Hotspur was a result that Sheffield Wednesday needed, not simply to get a win under their belt, but to re-kindle the confidence within the side. It certainly did prove beneficial, as between that September 13th victory and a 1-1 draw against Manchester United at Old Trafford on November 8th, some ten fixtures, six were won and four drawn, propelling the name of Sheffield Wednesday from twenty-second in the table to a heady ninth. Dooley was back amongst the goals, netting five of his team's sixteen, but the name 'Quixall' had still to appear amongst the scorers.

Was this a concern? Who knows. If Albert had been asked, he would have simply shrugged his shoulders and commented *"as long as the team's winning..."* Although there were no goals, his overall contribution continued to be immense and Ferrier's clarion call of mid-September was carried on by others, like a baton in a relay race, with the nation's sports writers almost all being of the opinion that a forthcoming international, and not a relatively minor Football League one, should see the name 'Quixall' up for contention.

"*Quixall (19) certain to get England selection soon*" was the headline in the *Daily Herald* on Monday October 13th, with Clifford Webb writing: "*Far too much caution is being displayed these days by selectors. A case in point is that of Albert Quixall, the brilliant Sheffield Wednesday inside forward, who has not yet been found a place in the England 'B' team.*

"*Young Albert, three weeks past his nineteenth birthday, dazzled fans at Highbury on Saturday and drew this frank comment from Tom Whittaker – "Quixall is the best inside forward I have seen for years. The boy's got everything"*'

"*Quixall who was born within a mile of the Wednesday ground and was a terrace fan at Hillsborough before he became a schoolboy international, is an apprentice joiner. His National Service call-up has been deferred until he is twenty-one.*

"*I am giving you these facts now because it seems obvious, we are going to see and hear a lot about Quixall.*

"*England's team manager, Walter Winterbottom, watched him at Highbury and my guess is that young Albert will get into the FA team against the RAF at Chelsea on October 22 and might easily have a very quick jump into the full England side.*"

Twenty-four hours after Webb's article appeared, the journalist was proved correct and Albert's name was included in the FA side to face the RAF. "*Quixall In FA Team*", "*Quixall Gets His Big Chance*" and "*A Cap Try-Out For Quixall?*" were amongst the headlines in the sports sections of the national press on October 14th. OK, it wasn't England or England 'B,' but it was a selection not to be shunned as it was a foot in the door, another rung on the footballing ladder climbed.

The Saturday prior to the announcement of his selection, Sheffield Wednesday had been in London, facing Arsenal at Highbury and the often fickle, highly critical, sports writers based in the capital had warmed to Albert's display. One in particular, Peter Campling of the *Daily News* being of the opinion that Jackie Sewell, the game's most expensive player, who kicked every ball from his seat in the Highbury stand, having been dropped by manager, Eric Taylor, would be wondering if he will ever regain his place in the Wednesday line-up due to the man who had taken his place – Albert Quixall.

The number ten jersey had been Albert's up until the Stoke City fixture at the Victoria Ground on October 4th, but with Sewell on England duty, Albert was handed the number eight shirt, renewing his partnership with Alan Finney on the right flank, which in turn brought about an immediate understanding, not to mention two points from a 3-1 victory following two 1-1 draws. With the performance considered much improved than that of recent weeks, Dooley getting back amongst the goals with a double, there was little chance of Taylor putting his head on the block and incurring the wrath of the supporters by re-juggling a winning side, so Sewell, much to his disappointment saw himself out in the cold.

But back in his native Yorkshire, Richard Ulyatt, writing in the *Yorkshire Post and Leeds Intelligencer*, following the Arsenal fixture, although admitting that he was: *"perhaps the most promising young forward in the country"* was to add: *"I had hoped that he would be allowed to mature more slowly, even in Wednesday's reserve team, for as yet he appears to me to tire after an hour's exacting football."* There was just no pleasing some.

That blue and white striped Wednesday shirt was exchanged for the white of England, or to be more exact, the Football Association and Albert headed off to Stamford Bridge to face a strong R.A.F. side that contained the likes of Mudie of Blackpool, Edwards of Bolton Wanderers, Broadbent and Flowers of Wolves and Hubbard of Glasgow Rangers, the eleven that was considered by some to be somewhat superior to that of the FA Side. Amongst Albert's team mates were Willemse of Chelsea, Kennedy and Barlow of West Bromwich Albion and Swinbourne and Wilshaw of Wolves. If the R.A.F. side was indeed superior, then they failed to show it in the 8-1 defeat.

Well covered in the national press, there was little doubting who took the laurels from their performance across the ninety minutes.

"But star forward afield was Sheffield Wednesday's 19-year-old inside right Albert Quixall. Simply tireless and always creating openings, he scored two of the goals and had a hand in three others. He must be reckoned among our outstanding prospects" – *Birmingham Daily Gazette*.

"*Quixall Now Ready For England*" was the headline above Charles Buchan's match report for the *London Daily News*, and here was a man who knew what he was talking about. "*Fair-haired 19-year-old inside right Albert Quixall of Sheffield Wednesday is a certain England cap of the future. Two-footed, quick thinking, clever with the ball and supremely confident, he reminded me of Wilf Mannion when the Middlesbrough man first started on the road to fame.*

"*Quixall was the outstanding player of the game. He scarcely made a bad pass, was always in position, and had that valuable asset of quick acceleration that deceives opposition and leads to goals.*

"*Quixall is so mature he is ready for a place in England's team to meet Wales at Wembley on November 12.*"

"*Quixall Genius*" proclaimed the *Belfast News-Letter* – "*This player was responsible for the FA teams runaway victory over the R.A.F.*"

The *Daily Mirror* – "*Quixall Leads Rout*" – "*Albert Quixall, the fair-haired boy who is keeping the £34,000 Jackie Sewell inside right out of the Sheffield Wednesday team, strengthened his claims to succeed Sewell as England inside right yesterday. His flair for combining artistry with punch made him the outstanding figure in the FA XI's 8-1 victory over the RAF at Chelsea. He scored two goals, and engineered the openings for most of the others. Quixall is only nineteen, yet in this fiasco of a football match he displayed the skill, poise and assurance of Wilf Mannion.*

"*The 6,000 crowd took Quixall to their hearts, applauding his passes, laughing at his tricks and groaning when he hit the post with a hat-trick effort.*"

So, two comparisons to Wilf Mannion, while Clifford Webb of the *Daily Herald* likened him to another footballing legend – Alex James. Below the heading "*Albert Quixall Has Alex James Touch,*" Webb wrote: "*Almost single-handed little Albert Quixall, apprentice joiner and master footballer, shot down the RAF at Stamford Bridge yesterday when the FA XI beat the flying boys 8-1.*

"*This fair-haired, stockily-built inside right from Sheffield Wednesday seems destined to become England's favourite footballer.*

"*In this his first representative match, dazzled as the smartest looking all-round prospect since Herbert Chapman picked out Alex James at Preston.*

"*The 19-year-old schoolboy international produced a display that was an amazing mixture of skill, speed and shooting ability, cracked two of the eight goals himself – and they were just about the best of the bunch – and had a working part in four of the others.*"

"*Spellbound by the genius of Albert Quixall,*" "*A natural ball-player, Quixall already moves like a man with years of experience in big football.*" And so it continued, with Richard Ulyatt's assessment that he tired after an hour, coming back to haunt him.

Albert's outstanding performance was perhaps not surprising to those who had stood on the vast Hillsborough terraces and watched him through what was still a somewhat brief career. But it was also a performance that presented those faceless England selectors with a problem, although they did have a week in which to decide what the outcome would be.

England were due to face Wales at Wembley on November 12th, while an FA XI was due to tackle the Army seven days prior to that. Normally it would be a case of the best eleven, injuries permitting and all bias put aside, to face Wales, whilst the also-rans facing the Army. All, however, was far from clear-cut.

In the previous England international against Northern Ireland at the beginning of October, they had struggled to an unconvincing 2-2 draw in Belfast. Over the course of the following month much had changed due to circumstances in the steel city of Sheffield.

At inside right for England, in Belfast, was Jackie Sewell, football's most expensive individual. His place in the Wednesday side being taken by a certain Albert Quixall, Wednesday had flourished. Sewell, was not missed in the slightest, and was now unable to regain his place in the Wednesday starting line-up. Furthermore, the R.A.F. Had struggled against a Quixall-inspired FA XI.

The multitude cried: *"Quixall for England,"* but some, like the Bob Ferrier of the *Daily Mirror* spoke of caution, admitting that there was certainly room for young players to come through and bolster our international prestige, but at the same time should not demand immediate places for them in the starting line-up. He added that the fixture against Wales would be *"a football furnace and no place for a youngster like Quixall. Far better the selectors to continue with the Quixall apprenticeship with a place in the Leeds match. The Army will probably provide stiffer opposition than did the R.A.F. team. Quixall might well have a place in the match against Belgium, if he maintains his form, two weeks after the Wales match, but not Wales, if you please, gentlemen."*

But Ferrier wasn't alone in his thoughts, as Jack Peart of the *Sunday Mirror* echoed his thoughts saying that Albert's inclusion in the England side for the forthcoming fixture against Wales was: *"Not for my money,"* adding *"This is no uncharitable after-thought, merely an appeal to reason now that the tumult and the shouting have died. Frankly, Quixall is not ready yet. Quixall is good. One day he may be great; but let's keep our sense of proportion. It would be unfair to thrust this comparatively inexperienced youngster into the toughest match on our international programme."*

Ferrier and Peart's comments could well be considered as being totally unfounded. The Welsh side, were far from being some foreign eleven, whose tactical attributes were totally alien to the English game, who would often adopt a 'win at all cost' attitude and cared little for reputations, or for that matter age. The Welsh eleven would be most probably individuals who Albert had faced in League fixtures, a mixture of players from the likes of Cardiff City, Swansea, Manchester City and Newcastle United. Yes, international football was played on a different field with national pride to play for, but the promotion and relegation struggles could conjure up much more physical encounters.

As the "yes he should" "no he shouldn't" debate flourished, there was little need to put Albert Quixall under a microscope, as everyone knew what they would discover, and no optical instrument was required to know that here was a young player who was no passing flight of fancy, but one who could only improve as he continued to mature.

The ability of individuals can often be judged in some quarters as hinging on bias, but while Bob Ferrier was one individual who showed little hint of this, in fact the exact opposite is true in his case, there was certainly no bias when it came to reporting the English game from the opposite side of Hadrian's Wall, but even members of the Scottish press-pack had been charmed by the play of Sheffield Wednesday's up and coming starlet. The esteemed 'Waverley' of the *Daily Record* was to write that he had been in London and standing at Earls Court Station en route for Stamford Bridge and that FA v R.A.F. fixture when he encountered Jimmy Easson a former Dundee and Portsmouth player, who was now on the training staff of the latter. *"Keep a close eye on the England 'B' team inside right, Quixall,"* he was advised.

"I did," 'Waverley' penned, *"and I hereby prophesy that this well-built, fair-haired lad will come to be a menace to Scotland's chances of victory in our games with England in the future. Indeed, I would say that he should be brought in right away.*

"He scored two lovely goals in the FA team's 8-1 win, but, what is more important, he played soccer from the inside forward's point of view, with the class that made such as Mannion and Carter the great players they have been against Scotland."

'Waverley's' appraisal didn't quite finish there, as, a few days later, he mentioned that Albert had been the talk of football since those ninety minutes against the R.A.F, whilst commenting on Jackie Sewell's Wednesday predicament. *"I have lost my place in the Wednesday side because I played for England,"* Sewell had said. *"But I did not think that policy was to operate more or less indefinitely."*

What was surprising was the fact that no path had been beaten towards the doors of Hillsborough by club chairmen with cheque books in hand, no words of warning from the Wednesday directorate shouting *"hands off our Albert."* That, however, soon changed.

Monday October 22nd produced the headline in the *Birmingham Daily Gazette*: *"£20,000 Albion Cheque Ready For Right Man." "West Bromwich Albion are ready to pay £.20,000, possibly more, for an inside forward. But he must be good, young and a man who will put club first,"* began the article that followed, going on to add that the club was looking for an individual who could help them towards achieving championship success, a player, ideally aged around twenty-one who could give the club a playing career of around ten years.

Albion weren't blind, nor stupid for that matter, they had their sights on Albert Quixall, and the approach was made. *"We would like to buy Quixall,"* uttered the straight-to-the-point Albion. *"That's all right with us,"* came the reply. *"How much?"* responded Albion. *"£60,000."* Taken aback, Albion officials then asked about Jackie Sewell and were told that he would cost the same as Wednesday had paid for him, round £34,000. They left empty-handed, although it was thought that they might return for Albert with an extra £5,000. Time would tell.

The question on everyone's lips, however: "was Albert Quixall worth £60,000?" In a nutshell, no. Despite this precocious talent being the the talk of the sport's columns, the figure quoted had simply been plucked out of thin air, a sum of money that was laughable if it weren't serious, a figure mentioned to put West Bromwich Albion off and deter anyone else from making enquiries about a player that Sheffield Wednesday had no intentions of losing.

But then, on the other hand, was he a better player than Sewell for whom Wednesday broke the bank, or indeed, was Sewell worth the money that sealed his transfer? In hindsight, no, and as recent weeks had shown, Albert Quixall was a much better option than the England international, so in general terms, was worth more than that £30-£35,000 fee.

Wednesday had set the bar high, in a period where football, like life itself was still finding its feet again following the trauma of the Second World War. In those immediate post-war years, it was teams like Liverpool, Portsmouth, Manchester United, Arsenal, their north London neighbours Tottenham Hotspur, and Wolverhampton Wanderers who ruled the roost in the First Division, while others like Newcastle United and Charlton Athletic could lay claim to FA Cup success. Money, however, was still tight, and Wednesday could perhaps be grateful that they could splash cash on the likes of Sewell, whilst not being up there amongst the leading clubs. That Second Division title of 1951-52 was their first since the 1920's when they claimed that same honour in 1925-

26, followed by successive First Division titles in 1928-29 and 1929-30. Albert Quixall was now the jewel in their crown, but for how long?

With the R.A.F. having borne the brunt of Albert Quixall's all-round ability, it was only natural that he gave the Army a similar taste of his medicine, and, on Monday November 5th 1952, he was the schemer-in-chief behind his FA team's 4-1 victory over a strong Army side at Leeds United's Elland Road.

A few days later, he was switched to the inside-left position in the Wednesday side, as the simmering frustration of Jackie Sewell, which had been expected to boil over with every passing day, was finally dispelled when he was restored to the line-up for the trip to Old Trafford to face Manchester United. The move, although failing to produce a victory, extended Wednesday's nine game unbeaten run into double figures, but it was to end a run of four consecutive victories.

A further seven days down the line, what was tagged as the 'Wednesday odd-man out plan' conjured up the headline – *"Quixall Dropped For The First Time,"* as he was left out for the visit of Portsmouth to Hillsborough. It wasn't, of course, the first occasion that Albert had not found his name included in the first team listing prior to a game, but it was the first this season.

Was it rotation that actually saw Albert's name missing from that Wednesday line-up to face Portsmouth, or was it simply a case of keeping Jackie Sewell happy, manager Eric Taylor not wanting to rock the boat, or see his big money signing demand a transfer, and if a move materialised, most probably see him sold at a loss. Everyone had their thoughts and opinions and, by tea time that Saturday afternoon, Taylor may well have been regretting his actions as Wednesday had lost another of those 'seven goal thrillers' 4-3. The slide down the table, although not at avalanche speed, but worrying nevertheless, continued.

Having been omitted from the Wednesday side to face Portsmouth, there was some concern surrounding Albert's immediate future. Not that he was on the verge of asking for a transfer to another club, but there was a transfer of a kind about to appear on the horizon, as, the day prior to that Portsmouth fixture, he had undergone his medical examination in the wake of his call-up for National Service.

It was expected that he would be joining the Royal Engineers, although not until after Christmas, but once he was enlisted and unquestionably drafted into the world of Army football, they would have priority over his selection for any future games should they clash with any Sheffield Wednesday fixtures and, although he was a signed Hillsborough professional, the club would have to go cap in hand and ask for his release if, and when, they required his services.

Omitted from the Wednesday starting line-ups to face Bolton Wanderers and Aston Villa as November drew to a close, Albert returned to first team action against Sunderland on December 6th in the completely alien position of outside-left, only requiring a run-out at centre-forward to complete the full set of selection in all five forward positions. It was not, however, to be a happy return, as the Roker Park side clinched victory by the odd goal in three.

An injury to Sewell saw Albert return to his favoured inside-right position for the visit of Wolves on December 13th, but it was again to no avail, as Wednesday slumped to another defeat, 3-2, pushing them further into the bottom half of the First Division. That dark cloud, however, surprisingly dispersed the following week when Newcastle United, who were on a six-game winning streak, were beaten 5-1 at St James's Park, but it was a victory that Albert did not participate in, as he was sidelined with an injury and didn't appear again in the Wednesday first team until the New Year.

With his National Service call-up date having hung in the air in recent weeks, he was finally given notice that he had to report to Catterick on January 17th and join the Royal Engineers as expected. He was also given a clean bill of health on the injury front, so was recalled to the Wednesday starting line-up against Middlesbrough as January reared its head. He kept his place for the visit of Cardiff City to Hillsborough two days later, which was to be his final appearance until January 31st when some unexpected leave allowed him to turn out for Wednesday's Central League side against Manchester City at Hillsborough.

Looking towards the new year of 1953, sports writers, with column inches to fill, took to naming who they considered to be the most promising prospects for the next twelve months. George Whiting of the *Londonderry Sentinel* had no doubts that *"a youngster who was beginning to look the double of Wilf Mannion, in both appearances and performance must catch the eye."* He went on to add: *"On the field, Quixall has that essential cheek that betokens confidence and poise, a nimble player with superb ball control and remarkable reactions that show his thirst for goal and sharp accurate passing."*

He was certainly not going to lose any of those attributes whilst doing his National Service and faced with arguably a greater fitness regime, he would more than likely return to Wednesday a much stronger and improved individual. His time at Catterick, would have been considered far from ideal, but the vast majority of those who endured that period in uniform simply took it on board as being part of the growing up process. For the sports minded individuals, it may well have been considered something of a holiday in disguise, and in the case of No. 22762676 Signalman Quixall A., he had to wait only a matter of weeks before being selected for the Army side to face Scotland at Hampden on March 2nd.

The tug of war between the Army and Sheffield Wednesday had begun and it couldn't have come at a worse time for the latter, as January had produced only one victory – 2-0 at Hillsborough against Cardiff City, a 2-2 draw at Middlesbrough and three consecutive defeats against Charlton Athletic, Tottenham Hotspur and Wolverhampton Wanderers, with a further 2-1 FA Cup defeat at home to Blackpool thrown in for good measure. Those three successive League defeats soon became four when Burnley returned home across the Pennines on the back of a 4-2 victory the first Saturday in February. The presence of Albert in the Wednesday line-up between January 17th and February 7th was sorely missed, but even when he returned for the journey to Preston North End on February 14th, having finally managed to obtain leave, it mattered little, as the struggle for momentum and points continued, a solitary goal being enough to give the home side victory. It was now five League fixtures without a victory, but by some manner of means, Wednesday remained in twelfth place, the same position they had found themselves in back in December following their 5-1 victory over Newcastle United. To make matters worse, with the Preston North End game still very much in the balance and the crowd awaiting that opening goal, they were stunned into relative silence on the hour mark when Derek Dooley went down under a challenge from Thompson and was carried off on a stretcher with what was later revealed to be a break just below the knee.

As Dooley left the Deepdale pitch on that stretcher and was immediately whisked off to hospital, no-one, not even the player himself realised the serious predicament he was about to find himself in. Two days after his admission to hospital, it became clear that he was suffering from much more than a broken leg, as a statement released from Preston Royal Infirmary on the Tuesday afternoon said. *"Dooley's injury has been complicated by a dangerous type of infection and an emergency operation was performed last night. His condition remains grave."* It was also revealed that at 4.23 a.m. an SOS had been sent out to other hospitals for an anti-gangrene serum and an hour and nine minutes later it arrived via a police car from Blackrod, who had picked it up from another police car that had originally collected it from Manchester Royal Infirmary. Given the injections within an hour, it was hoped to have been enough to aid Dooley's recovery, but unfortunately, it wasn't and the orthopaedic surgeon at Preston Infirmary was left with no option than to amputate his leg just above the knee. He was only twenty-three.

With sixteen goals to his credit, the absence of Dooley was to be a severe blow to Wednesday, adding even more pressure on their fight to maintain First Division status. Having to fight the Army to obtain the services of Albert only added to the concern, as did the constant worry with regards to Albert remaining injury-free as he continued his playing career with the Army and whatever England eleven he was selected for.

Football was Albert Quixall's life and whilst on his National Service, he was ensured plenty of it. Four days after turning out for Wednesday against Preston North End, he was back in Lancashire, turning out for the Corps of Signals against Manchester University at Fallowfield, where he got himself on the score sheet.

Just how Albert kept track of his footballing career leaves one wondering, as he would have required a diary to keep a note of where he would be and when. Sheffield Wednesday's fixtures were more or less written in stone, but then there was the Army XI and his unit within that Army set-up, while the England selectors decided that he would be included in the England 'B' side to face Scotland 'B' in what was the first meeting between the two countries at such a level and something that would become an annual fixture.

There had been much debate over the selection of individuals on national service, but the general opinion in Albert's case was that it would have been something of an injustice if he wasn't selected.

First up in the Quixall diary was a trip to Scotland to play for the Army against the national side at Hampden on Monday March 3rd, ninety minutes that was to produce something of a lacklustre display from the visitors.

Alongside the likes of John Bond of West Ham United, Ronnie Clayton of Blackburn Rovers and Vic Keeble of Newcastle United, Albert was subdued by the hard tackling Dundee defender, Doug Cowie, over the course of the first forty-five minutes, so much so that he switched flanks for the second half, moving from indie-right to inside left, but still couldn't inspire his team to victory, the home side winning by the odd goal in three. He was, however, picked out as the star man in an undistinguished Army side. *"Only Quixall looked as if he could marshal an Army offensive,"* penned one reporter covering the game, although Colin Glenn of the *Dundee Courier* wrote that he *"spoiled a lot of good work by being a bit cocky with his team mates."*

Just over a week later, on March 11th, he came face to face with Doug Cowie once again as they lined up for that inaugural 'B' international fixture at Easter Road, Edinburgh, a game that finished all-square at two goals apiece. Both sides contained names that remain familiar today – Ronnie Simpson, then of Newcastle United, was between the sticks for the home side, who were captained by Tommy Docherty. Charlton's John Hewie, and Ian McMillan who was to find fame with Rangers, but was then with Airdrie, could also be found in a dark blue jersey. As for England there was the likes of Roger Byrne of Manchester United, Jimmy Adamson of Burnley, Ray Barlow of West Bromwich Albion alongside Albert, who was considered by the press not to fair too well and was hardly in the game over the course of the ninety minutes. Some even suggested that he was far from ready for the main international stage.

Returning to Catterick, un-moved by the criticism, a quick look at the diary, Albert must have wondered how he could fit everything in. He did manage some breathing space, as Sheffield Wednesday's request for his presence in their side to face Blackpool on March 14th was refused, as the Army wanted the now lance-corporal Quixall for the 7th Training Battalion of the Royal Signals side to face R.O.A.C. Hilsea in the semi-final of the Army Cup at the Command Stadium, Aldershot on March 18th.

He was to return to camp with a smile on his face having made a major contribution to his team's 6-4 victory, scribbling yet another date into the diary: the Army Cup Final on April 15th against 28th Battalion (Bramley) R.O.A.C.

But before Albert could focus on that Cup Final appearance, he was given leave to report back to Sheffield Wednesday on March 21st, but was only to line-up in the Central League side against Bolton Wanderers. Then a week later, there was a Kentish Cup tie against the Belgian Army at Dulwich Hamlet, where he again enjoyed a favourable afternoon in a 2-1 win.

As he travelled the length and breadth of the county with his Army colleagues, there is no doubt whatsoever that Albert kept in touch with the goings on back at Hillsborough and would have been disappointed that Wednesday were dropping closer and closer to the relegation zone in the First Division, something that he was helpless to prevent. As the penultimate month of the season drew to a close with a 0-0 draw at Old Trafford against Manchester United, a quick glance at the table would show seven clubs below Sheffield Wednesday, but a closer examination revealed that there were in fact five clubs, alongside Wednesday, on thirty-one points, then three on twenty-nine and one on twenty-eight. Bottom club Derby County already looked down and out on twenty-five.

So, April beckoned and oh, how Sheffield Wednesday craved the presence of their young inside forward. Good Friday took them to Maine Road, with the 3-1 defeat at the hands of Manchester City pushing them down to seventeenth. Twenty-four hours later, the long trip to Portsmouth, with Albert re-installed in the line-up, brought a further drop, down to eighteenth, following a 5-2 defeat. The difference of an Albert Quixall Sheffield Wednesday and one without could be argued, as, despite the crushing defeat, Albert notched his only goal of the season. Who is to say that had it not been for National Service, Wednesday's position could have been much different, and the 1-1 draw on Easter Monday in the return fixture against Manchester City could have seen two points gained instead of the one.

In a matter of days, Wednesday's position had become precarious, only two points separated the Hillsborough side, Middlesbrough, Stoke City and Chelsea. Derby still lagged five behind. What made matters worse was, that while Wednesday had thirty-two points from their thirty-nine games, Middlesbrough, also on thirty-two, Stoke, on thirty-one and Chelsea on thirty had all played a game less. Having hit the heady heights of eighth back in November in that nine-match unbeaten run, Wednesday had found themselves on something of a downward spiral ever since.

Blocking his club's predicament from his mind the best he could, Albert headed back to Aldershot on April 15th for the Army Cup Final against 28th Battalion R.A.O.C. (Bramley), where the biggest post-war crowd for the fixture saw the Catterick side lift the trophy with a 3-2 victory.

A goal up in twenty-five minutes, an Albert Quixall free-kick from twenty-five yards out, set the mood for the game and the Signals were 2-0 ahead five minutes later. Undeterred, the Ordnance side rallied and pulled a goal back five minutes before the break, but with fifteen minutes remaining they were to find themselves once again two goals behind. Two minutes from time, Keeble of Newcastle pulled a goal back for the Ordnance side, but it was too late to salvage anything from the game and Albert and his team mates returned north with the trophy, won for the first time, and their winners medals.

From Aldershot and a cup final to Villa Park, Birmingham and a relegation fight three days later was the mixed-up football world of Albert Quixall in April 1953, as he, or at least Sheffield Wednesday, had gained leave for him to assist the Yorkshire side in their final one hundred and eighty minutes of the season. But despite being granted leave, would he be running out of the Hillsborough tunnel, or the one at Wembley in the white of England?

The importance of having him back in a blue and white striped shirt could not be denied, but Fred Walters of the *Green 'Un* found the case of Albert Quixall *"Difficult To Understand."* He wrote: *"It will always be difficult to understand how it is that an inside forward like Quixall can play twenty-four games and score only one goal. This was not the style of football that made him one of the outstanding schoolboy players of a few years ago. No wonder those schoolmasters who took an interest in him in those days are at a loss to understand him now.*

"These are matters that will have to be remedied another season in what I still hope will be the First Division."

Could it be Wednesday's style of play, pushing Albert back to behind the main front men? Was the knowledge that the other teams, and their defenders, had of his capabilities, generating a close man-marking tactic? Who knows? But it was certainly not seen as a problem by the player himself, as he found the net, although not overly frequently in his representative games for country and the Army.

Some were also of the opinion that the lack of goals had hindered his England selection at full international level, but despite the concerns of Fred Walters and countless others as regards the lack of goals, whenever international football reared its head, Albert's name was always at the forefront and it was no different as the annual meeting between the 'Auld Enemy' of England and Scotland loomed on the horizon, ironically the same afternoon that Wednesday were to lock horns with Aston Villa.

One of the journalists in the *London Daily News* was the highly respected, former Arsenal player, Charles Buchan, who had asked eleven former England internationalists to select a team in their old position to face the Scots. The 'forward line' consisted of Sammy Crooks (Derby County), David Jack (Arsenal), George Camsell (Middlesbrough), Billy Walker (Aston Villa) and Eric Houghton (Aston Villa). Matthews, Lofthouse, Froggatt and Finney were four of the five chosen, with David Jack rounding off the front line by selecting *"Albert Quixall – The best inside right I have seen for a long time."* Buchan and the England selectors, however, were still not convinced with Albert's credentials and once again he was omitted from the England starting line-up.

So, it was to be Hillsborough, not Wembley, where Albert found himself on the afternoon of April 18th 1953, where there were to be goals in abundance, although once again, the name Quixall failed to appear amongst them, as did a Sheffield Wednesday victory, with Villa returning to the Midlands on the back of a 4-3 win. Despite failing to score, although he was denied by the keeper on more than one occasion, he was considered to have had an outstanding game. No matter what, that defeat meant the grim reaper was staring Sheffield Wednesday firmly between the eyes.

The odds were stacked against Wednesday's First Division survival and a close study of the table and remaining fixtures following that defeat at the hands of Aston Villa did not make good reading for anyone connected with the Hillsborough club, the bottom half dozen looking as follows: 17th – Stoke City: Pd. 41. Pts. 34. Still to play Derby at home. 18th – Liverpool: Pd. 40. Pts. 34. Still to play Chelsea at home and Manchester United away. 19th – Chelsea: Pd. 40. Pts. 33. Still to play Liverpool away and Manchester City at home. 20th – Sheffield Wednesday: Pd. 41. Pts. 33. Still to play Sunderland at home. 21st – Manchester City: Pd. 39. Pts. 33. Still to play Preston and Blackpool at home and Chelsea away. 22nd – Derby: Pd. 40. Pts. 30. Still to play Stoke away and Preston at home.

Wednesday's predicament was by far the worst, their First Division future lay in the hands of others, although victory over Sunderland was vital.

The Hillsborough terraces swayed in anticipation and they took the lead in the 12th minute through Sewell. Twice Albert brought groans from the crowd as he failed to make the most of scoring opportunities that came his way, but on the half-hour mark he made amends of sorts when he jumped for the ball alongside Aitken, his presence forcing the Villa defender to head into his own goal.

Three minutes into the second half, Sewell scored a third, his hat-trick being completed a minute and a half later, accepting a pass from Albert before giving Threadgold in the Villa goal no chance with his shot. Albert himself should have added a fifth. Running clear down the middle, he shot two yards wide with only the keeper to beat. Fortunately, it mattered little.

That victory saw Wednesday leap to 17th, their now total of thirty-five points ensuring that Hillsborough would witness First Division football for another season at least.

While the majority of his fellow professionals could throw their boots into the cupboard and forget about them for a couple of months, Albert had to keep the dubbin at hand and his boots polished, as he was off with his Army mates on a tour of Austria and Germany.

CHAPTER THREE
WEDNESDAY, THE ARMY AND ENGLAND AT LAST

Fitness was certainly something that Albert Quixall did not lack, especially since beginning his National Service, and, prior to the start of the 1953-54 season, he had endured, or enjoyed, a three-week Army P.T. course at Scarborough, so he was certainly well prepared for the season ahead. However, his season at League level was not the First Division hot-bed which he was now accustomed to, but the Central League, lining up against Preston North End at Deepdale on August 22nd.

Somewhat strangely, Sheffield Wednesday opened the First Division campaign with two home victories: 2-0 against Manchester City and 2-1 three days later against Tottenham Hotspur. The latter giving them pride of place at the top of the table, but that rare event was only momentary, as by the end of the month they were fifteenth, having lost 6-0 at Preston North End and 4-1 at Burnley. Nothing, however could detract from the harsh defeat at Deepdale, where Preston also missed two penalties, as Wednesday lost goalkeeper McIntosh after twenty minutes with a broken arm.

The dark clouds cleared from the sky as September got underway, with the 6-0 defeat at Preston being shown as no more than bad luck, as the return fixture at Hillsborough, again featuring six goals but on this occasion, four of them in Wednesday's favour. It was also to see Albert Quixall's name move from the Central League line-up back to that of the Wednesday first team, replacing the injured Sewell.

His performance against Preston was undoubtedly Albert Quixall at his best, making two of his team's goals. It even brought praise from Fred Walters of the *Green 'Un*, who at times was far from being Albert's biggest fan and often critical of his performances. However, in his column on Saturday September 5th he was to write: *"No one had been more critical of Quixall's style of play at times in the past than I have.*

"This was because I knew Quixall, from what I saw in his schooldays, to be capable of something far better than the style of football he had played with Wednesday on most occasions.

"In two games – those against Sunderland last May and Preston on Wednesday – he has shown his true ability. In these games he played as an inside forward should and to his own satisfaction – it does not take long to know whether he is doing justice to himself in a game – should encourage him to continue in this way."

But perhaps the problem was not Albert Quixall; could it not have been the inconsistency of Sheffield Wednesday, who went from the heights to the depths at the flick of a switch. National Service may also have taken something out of him: the travelling, the completely different training regime, along with the infrequency of being able to turn out for the Hillsborough side. Once that period of National Service was completed, there was more than the slightest possibility that the real Albert Quixall would come to the fore.

The inconsistency that Wednesday had seemingly adopted became all too obvious as September progressed. Having opened the season with the two victories, which in turn gave way to two reversals, followed by that 4-2 win over Preston, the next three fixtures, at home to Charlton Athletic and away to Bolton Wanderers and neighbours Sheffield United all resulted in defeats.

Albert's performance against Preston, which was seen on the whole as considerably improved, was not continued into those next three games.

Despite his inconsistency, running in parallel with that of his club, Albert was selected for the Football League side to face their Irish counterparts in Belfast on Wednesday September 23rd, a selection that saw Clifford Webb write in the *Daily Herald*: *"This Belfast affair is not, of course, an international match, but if Quixall looks the part he is certain to go into the England side for the first World Cup preliminary – against Wales at Cardiff on October 10th.*

"The boy is a "natural." He is a high stepper in the Peter Doherty tradition, a beautiful mover, a great ball-player and a pusher-out o' perfect passes.

"People have told me that Albert is bit up in the clouds because of the praise which has been heaped upon him from an early age.

"If he can do all he is needed do, both for the Football League and, later, for England, that won't matter.

"Quixall's debut in a game of this kind, surrounded by colleagues with much more experience, is something the majority of us have been waiting impatiently to see."

His selection for the Football League against the Irish League, despite recent form and his omission from the Wednesday side on occasion, was to prove totally justified, as he captured the headlines in the 5-0 rout. *"Quixall Schemes Towards First Cap"* was the headline above Charles Buchan's match report in the *London Daily News*, with the Sunderland and Arsenal legend writing: *"Albert Quixall, the 20-year-old Sheffield Wednesday inside right, stole the honours of a runaway Football League victory at Windsor Park, Belfast, last evening.*

"Not only did he partner Tom Finney like a seasoned campaigner, but by intelligent positioning, provided the link between attack and defence that has so often been missing in representative teams.

"Even allowing for the moderate opposition of the Irishmen, gallant triers but hopelessly outclassed, Quixall earned a place in the English team for the match with Wales at Cardiff on October 10."

"He's arrived." proclaimed Clifford Webb in the *Daily Herald*: *"The Sheffield boy has undoubtedly arrived to give the go-ahead look to the front line. He was quick and strong – a rare mixture of storming attacker and cool distributor.*

"As a partner to the unpredictable Tom Finney he was seldom in the wrong.

"To the big question – is Quixall ready? – I would answer an emphatic 'Yes' "

Following his success in the white of the Football League in Belfast it was straight back into his Army colours for a match against Everton at Goodison Park, but he could do little to help his team avoid a 6-2 defeat. Speculation was now rife that finally a call-up to the senior England side was in sight.

Whenever and wherever Albert Quixall played, he was the centre of attention. Be it his excellent vision when it came to picking out a team mate with an exquisite pass, his mane of blonde hair, his diminutive stature, or his passion for hoisting his shorts up his thighs in comparison to the 'baggy' style of the majority, he stood out in the crowd. Regarding the shorts, he was to say: *"I like to play with my shorts hitched up around my waist. The purpose is not to make myself distinctive but merely to give more freedom to my legs."* It was, however, a look that did not go down well with the Army.

Prior to the meeting with Everton, he was given strict instructions to wear regulation shorts, or more to the point, wear them the same way as his team mates. Adhered to at this level, it was back to the norm when he turned out for Sheffield Wednesday who were more lenient and no sticklers for detail.

It was all ears to the radio on Monday October 5th 1953 when the England team to face Wales at Cardiff the following Saturday was announced and it was hardly a surprise when his name was mentioned amongst the eleven. There would most probably have been an outcry had it not. But it had to be remembered that he was just out of his teens and five years previously had been playing for the England Schools side. Against that, he had added the experience of some fifty League appearances, two England 'B' caps and one for the Football League. One analysis following his selection mentioned that he was currently in Aldershot on yet another P.T. course, with fifteen months of his National Service still to run, adding that he was *"extremely strong and clever, he is a constructive type of player but one who does not conform to any set pattern. If the mood strikes him, he will roam to the other side of the field or shoot through in a long solo raid on goal. He is always wanting the ball and never happier than when it is front of him."*

As the days until that England debut drew nearer, a doubt suddenly materialised in Albert's mind that he might miss his dream date when he developed a slight inflammation of the throat, but twenty-four hours prior to the Wales fixture, he was declared fit to play, much to his relief.

In the reports that followed England's far from emphatic 4-1 victory, the name Quixall was prominent throughout

But it was four days after the encounter that Bob Ferrier penned in the *Daily Mirror*: *"The England soccer selectors are in danger of making a grievous mistake. They meet today to pick a team to play against F.I.F.A at Wembley next Wednesday, and I believe they may leave Albert Quixall, the young team Sheffield Wednesday inside right, out of the team.*

"If they do this, they might shatter the future of the finest inside forward to emerge for England since the war. It has happened with other players who never quite recovered from being dropped after one selection.

"Maybe it wouldn't happen to Quixall. I don't know, but I do know that the risk is not worth taking. Quixall is a gem to be polished regularly in international football."

From the international stage, it was off to the more spartan surroundings of Aldershot to play for the Army against Aston Villa, moving back into the half-back line, but the 3-2 defeat only proved that he would have been better utilised up-front, but it had been at his own request that he took a place in the half-back line.

Facing Wales was all very well, but if there had been progress made over the course of his whirlwind career to date, he had to be judged alongside top-class players, and the ideal opportunity to see if he ticked the right boxes occurred eleven days after that Home International fixture when England faced the Rest of the World at Wembley.

There was only one change in the England line-up that had faced Wales and it wasn't the omission of Albert Quixall, but that of his right-wing partner at Ninian Park – Tom Finney, left out of the side for the first time in six years, save for the odd miss through injury. In his place came Stanley Matthews, twenty-one years since he began playing and eighteen years after his first cap. Bob Ferrier of the *Daily Mirror*, unconcerned about the leaving out of Finney or the inclusion of Matthews, wrote of Albert's presence: *"If they had left out Quixall they would have crucified the greatest England post-war find. Here is a gem of a player who, if properly polished will serve England for ten years."*

Tom Finney's omission, however, was fodder for the sporting press, eager to pounce on any titbits that came their way, or create a mountain out of a molehill, which was what they did with the Preston man's demotion from the England squad.

If the press were to be believed, then Finney had taken offence to Albert's personality and overall play, the reason behind the partnership failing to gel against the Welsh, which the Preston plumber vehemently denied when speaking to Stan Halsey of the *Sunday Pictorial*.

"That is not only untrue, it is a plain rotten suggestion. To suggest that a player in an England shirt would let personal considerations stop him doing his best for his country is diabolical nonsense."

Halsey was also to reveal that Albert's place in the England side to face the Rest of the World had been cemented prior to the fixture against the Welsh, with a selector being quoted as saying that they felt *"to drop him after one chance might blight a unique soccer skill before it reaches full bloom."*

October 1953 revealed the contrasting world in which Albert Quixall now found himself, a situation that would never have even entered his wildest dreams as a schoolboy. The tug-of-war between Sheffield Wednesday and the Army now had England joining the fray, with the 22nd of the month having brought selection for the Northern Command against the Southern Command at Gloucester City in the Inter-Command Challenge Cup, while twenty-four hours previously he was to be walking out at Wembley with his England teammates to face the Rest of the World in what was the Football Association's 90th anniversary match, emerging from the Wembley tunnel to a packed 97,000 stadium.

It was a momentous occasion, and not just for England's young inside right, with the following representing their respective teams:

England – Merrick (Birmingham City), Ramsey (Tottenham Hotspur), Eckersley (Blackburn Rovers), Wright (Wolverhampton Wanderers), Ufton (Charlton Athletic), Dickinson (Portsmouth), Matthews (Blackpool), Mortenson (Blackpool), Lofthouse (Bolton Wanderers), Quixall (Sheffield Wednesday) and Mullen (Wolverhampton Wanderers).

Rest of the World – Zeman (Austria), Navarro (Spain), Hannappi (Austria), Cjakowski (Yugoslavia), Posipal (Germany), Ocwirk (Austria), Boniperti (Italy), Kubala (Spain), Nordahl (Sweden), Vukas (Yugoslavia) and Zebec (Yugoslavia), an eleven, who today will only be familiar to the game's historians.

Despite the unfamiliarity of the opposition, they held England to a 4-4 draw and, by all accounts, were the better of the two teams, with England considered fortunate to maintain their unbeaten home record against foreign opposition, only a disputed penalty keeping that record intact.

For Albert, it was to be a disappointing ninety minutes, doing little to suggest a longer run in the white shirt, his lack of shots at goal, nothing materialising until the second half, being widely criticised. Whether or not he was simply obeying orders, he appeared to have something of a 'give it to Stan' complex, sending the ball out towards the Blackpool man when he should have taken on the responsibility of taking a shot at goal when the opportunity was there.

In the aftermath of that ninety minutes and the game being digested by the media, only Eric Stanger of the *Yorkshire Post and Leeds Intelligencer* offered anything in the way of back-handed support for the England inside left, and it was not a case of supporting a fellow white rose county man. He wrote: *"The only way back to English Soccer supremacy is by showing superior skill. You may say, "But what about Quixall, he is a ball player and he has not yet been a success." That true. Quixall is still a lad and inside forward is not a lad's position, as I have said before. You require years on your back to be the complete inside forward. Quixall may yet be our finest inside forward since the war, but has still much to learn."* On the other hand, his now No.1 fan, Bob Ferrier of the *Daily Mirror* was emphatic in his opinion that the name 'Quixall' should remain in the England line-up. Clifford Webb of the *Daily Herald*, however, was to write that it would not be disastrous if Albert was omitted from the next couple of England fixtures, as he could quite easily re-emerge to face Scotland later in the season and for the tour of Yugoslavia and Hungary prior to the World Cup ties in Sweden.

To the surprise of many, he retained his place in the England side to face Ireland at Goodison Park the following month, albeit switching from inside left to his preferred inside-right position.

Once an individual of note is set on a pedestal, they are a sitting target for the knockers, becoming akin to an object at a fairground coconut shy. Age mattered little, so it was Albert Quixall who was set up as the latest target for those knockers, with Charles Sampson of the *Newcastle Sunday Sun* nudging everyone out of the way for that opening shot. In an article which was headed: *"England Team No Place For Quixall,"* he scribbled: *"Trust the England selectors to bludgeon an idea to death. When Albert Quixall, Sheffield Wednesday's blond 19-year-old budding soccer genius, was chosen to fill England's inside-right berth against Wales earlier in the season it was regarded as being in nature of an experiment. As events turned out, the experiment was not exactly an unqualified success.*

"Nothing daunted, the selectors pitted the obviously inexperienced Quixall against the cream of Continental football in their 90th anniversary match against F.I.F.A at Wembley. Again, it was evident that Quixall, although he possessed unusual gifts, was not quite ready for the task allotted to him.

"Were the selectors prepared to call a temporary halt to their efforts to cultivate and encourage genius? Oh, dear no! Having discovered what they considered to be another budding Mannion, England's nine-man selection committee were determined to persevere with him.

"So, despite his present deficiencies, Albert Quixall plays his third game for England when he lines up against Ireland at Goodison Park, Everton, on Wednesday.

"I can name four inside forwards who have better qualifications at the present time than Quixall. I maintain that the England team is no place for a youngster who is still completing his soccer education."

Jack Peart of the *Sunday Mirror* was equally bemused by Albert's selection, but had to wait until Sampson had used up all his ammunition: *"Quixall has the promise of greatness, nothing more. He lacks the experience to dictate the course of a game – and that's the hallmark of every outstanding inside forward I've ever known."*

He may well have had much to learn, but Albert Quixall was certainly putting in the shifts, honing his skills whenever possible and, twenty-four hours after pulling on that England shirt, he was in more spartan surroundings at Gloucester City, for that Northern Command v Southern Command cup tie. In the 2-0 defeat, he once again came under-fire for his lack of attacking play, although supplying numerous accurate passes.

It is easy to forget that Albert was still a Sheffield Wednesday player, as the Hillsborough side looked to gain some momentum in their often-precarious plight in the First Division. Being unable to call on his services week-in week-out was more than just a minor hindrance. Of their five October 1953 fixtures, he was to feature in only three, against Liverpool away on the 3rd, Blackpool away on the 17th and Portsmouth at home on the 24th. Chelsea at home on the 10th and Arsenal away on the 31st saw him missing. That quintet of fixtures produced a mixed bag of results, two wins, two draws and a defeat that was to leave Wednesday in ninth place in the table.

Albert's lack of goals was indeed a concern and difficult to put a finger on. He was certainly more of a creative player than a goal scorer, but even those ball-playing conjurers had to chip in with the share of goals. Not, as in Albert's case, one a season.

That solitary contribution for the 1953-54 season was to come on November 7th against Aston Villa at Hillsborough in the 3-1 victory in what was to be something of a bittersweet ninety minutes.

Nine minutes into the game, having dispensed with his lacklustre England performance, he opened the scoring. Gannon made a run of some thirty yards before being rather unceremoniously fouled. From the resulting free-kick, Wednesday won a corner and from Finney's flag kick, Albert headed home from six yards out.

The second half, with Wednesday 2-0 in front, saw Albert kicked in the head and carried off and, although he returned to the fray, he looked dazed, but managed to see out the ninety minutes. Manager Eric Taylor was to say: *"Albert came up a bit rocky – like a boxer who had taken a count of eight – and had to rest a while.*

"He went back to finish the game, and has been around to the ground this morning – not for treatment, but just to show us how completely he has recovered."

Three days prior to that first, and only goal, of the season, it was Army duty again, this time facing an FA XI at Newcastle's St James' Park, with the *Shields Daily News* being of the opinion that: *"Despite local interest in Jackie Milburn (Newcastle United) and Stan Anderson (Sunderland), the centre of attraction for most at the FA XI v Army match at St. James' Park this afternoon was Albert Quixall, Sheffield Wednesday's young England international."* Despite the fanfare, Albert was kept under a tight rein in his side's 3-1 defeat.

If Albert was affected by the negative press he had been receiving it didn't show, but it is difficult to imagine that such criticism didn't cause some inner turmoil, as he was still maturing both as a footballer and a person. Thankfully, he still maintained his sense of humour; who knows what would have happened had he kept everything bottled up inside, and his sometimes cheeky personality was clearly in evidence when the England players gathered at Southport prior to the World Cup match against Ireland at Goodison Park.

"*Hello, Dad,*" uttered the twenty-year-old blond-headed Sheffield lad upon meeting thirty-nine-year-old Stanley Matthews, who had won his first cap when his new right wing partner was a year old, and the Blackpool man was greeted in a similar fashion whenever the pair brushed shoulders. The Seasiders' wing-man simply grinned and took it in the same good-humoured spirit that it was delivered, with the duo combining well in training, waylaying any doubts that the age difference could well create a problem.

However, despite England's convincing 3-1 victory, the long-knives were again out for Albert Quixall, justified or not. The ninety minutes seemed to pass him by, the rapport between him and Matthews that had been developed on the training pitch deserted them during the ninety minutes and he struggled with the spadework expected from an inside forward. *"It seems fairly certain that the Sheffield youngster will require a few more years' schooling before he becomes international standard"* perhaps said it all.

Had he been haunted by the Goodison Park experience against Ireland, re-visiting the scene seven days later could have given him nightmares, but over the course of ninety minutes that would have left many scratching their heads, Albert, despite some barracking by the Liverpudlian crowd back, was amongst his Army mates, teased and taunted a Scottish FA XI that included the rock like figure of St Mirren's Willie Telfer in the heart of its defence, Laurie Reilly of Hibs and Celtic's Willie Fernie up-front. He even scored "a brilliant goal" in the 3-2 defeat.

But if that performance and result put a smile back on Albert's face, then it was soon removed by the news that he had been left out of the England side to face Hungary, mentioned in the *Liverpool Echo* as being *"the problem boy of recent England games."*

The unfamiliar surroundings of Hillsborough and First Division football were back in total focus as the final month of what had often been a stormy 1953 appeared on the calendars. Even towards the end of the month, the Christmas lights did nothing to lift the gloom.

A 2-1 victory over Cardiff City at home got December off to an ideal start, but from then on, it was downhill faster than a sledge on a snow-covered hill, as four straight defeats followed at the hands of Manchester City, Tottenham Hotspur and twice against Manchester United. The foot of the table was once again in full view as Wednesday sat in 17th spot, again thankful that there was always one team worse off than the others at the foot, on this occasion it was Liverpool, five points away.

There is no denying that Albert Quixall had the ability to become a first-class footballer. Many considered him to already to be one. However, there were two huge question marks, two items on the agenda which needed to be addressed whenever his name was mentioned, which was indeed frequently, and these were his lack of goals and his performances when he pulled on the white shirt of England. Both are difficult to dissect some seven decades down the line and one can only offer an opinion as to the shortage of goals alongside his name and those inept ninety minutes in white.

As regards goals, although there were not the infinite technical details employed in comparison to the modern game, the chess board football, players still had to adhere to their manager's advice and play to his required systems. Although, unlike the modern game, individuality and freedom of expression was not exactly frowned upon.

Perhaps Albert Quixall was asked to play a deeper role in the Sheffield Wednesday team than he preferred, concentrate on getting the ball to team mates who were more skilled and experienced in the art of goal scoring. There was also the added pressure of Wednesday's yo-yoing form and their often-poor defensive play, with Albert having to play a more demanding dog-eat-dog role in that midfield hot bed. Had he been with a more attack minded team (Derek Dooley aside), one with a stronger defensive record and who jousted with others at the top end of the table, instead of constantly looking over their shoulders at the opposite end, it may well have been different. Even under a different manager, those goals might well have materialised.

In respect of his international performances, few as they were, again there may well have been multiple reasons behind there being little to shout about from the rooftops. Here was a young player, confident in his own ability whilst being level-headed, and barely out of his teens, thrown into an environment awash with seasoned professionals. Paired with the elder statesmen of Finney and Matthews, he had every reason to be overawed. Perhaps they did find Albert not to their liking, keeping those thoughts well and truly hidden from the public eye. Perhaps they had informed him, in no uncertain terms, just how they wanted the ball played to them, failing to accept anything different, a task that he tried just that little bit too hard to fulfil, having a knock-on effect on his own natural play. There might also have been the possibility of being asked to perform something of a different role to normal, something that even a player longer in the tooth would have needed more time to adjust to.

There was also a third item often added to the agenda, with many being of the belief that Albert Quixall was "cocky" and "big-headed." This was something that he emphatically denied. *"I admit that I am ambitious and that I believe in myself. As for being a 'big-head', all I can say is that I know only too well that I have an awful lot to learn."*

Excuses are not being made, attempting to maintain that 'golden boy' image from becoming tarnished, but there had to be something, as his nine-out-of-ten performances with the Army were more often than not, praiseworthy and laced with goals.

As 1953 disappeared from view, something of a mixed year in the life of Albert Quixall, Sheffield Wednesday and England footballer, and as the bells rang out to herald in 1954, it was hoped that the shackles that he found around his ankles and the wearisome weight than that often fell upon his shoulders would be removed once and for all. As it was to turnout, January 1954 had much to be positive about. Alongside the negative ninety minutes in the 4-2 defeat against Charlton Athletic and the conceding of a further two goals against Sheffield United, the local neighbours across the city at Bramall Lane were defeated 3-1 in a replay of the Third Round of the FA Cup, after a first tie 1-1 draw. This saw Wednesday reach the Fourth Round for the first time since season 1948-49.

In that Fourth Round tie at the end of January, Chesterfield were beaten 4-2, again in a replay, following a 0-0 draw.

Those five January fixtures saw Albert feature in the Sheffield Wednesday side on each occasion, a run in the side that he had not enjoyed for some time due to his other commitments. Had the Army got their way, then he would have missed the Sheffield United replay as he was initially required for two Army Cup fixtures, at Catterick and Blandford.

There was, however, never any fear of him being dropped from the Army sides, be it his company eleven or the Northern Command, but it was often felt that he was being asked to play too much football, coupled with the travelling that was also required. Against Hull City on January 21st, five days after the First Division clash with Charlton Athletic and two days prior to the League fixture against Sheffield United, he was in action for the Northern Command against Hull City, showing his class in the opening forty-five minutes, but tiring in the second.

For a player who had failed to scale the heights with England, had a lack of goals to his name with Sheffield Wednesday, Albert could still be considered as being 'high profile.' As January weaved its way towards a close, he was featured alongside Alf Ramsey in the *Bristol Evening Post* in their 'ABC of Soccer's Top Men'. While a competition in the Children's Post section of the *Lancashire Evening Post* offered a photograph of him as a consolation prize in a 'Paint A Doily' competition (first prize in the senior and junior sections was a 5s postal order). Should you not want one of Albert, then you could have one of film star Glynis Johns! Wonder who those runners-up chose?

The Army and Sheffield Wednesday continued to play tug-of-war for Albert's services throughout February, with manager Eric Taylor winning 5-1, losing out on the 24th of the month when he had to re-adjust his front line to face Liverpool, with his inside forward in Glasgow to face Rangers at Ibrox.

Having Albert at his disposal certainly made life a lot easier and Wednesday certainly reaped the benefits, winning two of their four First Division fixtures, drawing one and losing the other. It also saw further progress being made in the FA Cup, 4-2 defeat of Chesterfield, Albert being the architect of the victory, and Everton being defeated 3-1 in Round Five in front of a packed 65,000 at Hillsborough.

Perhaps if Albert had been able to play against Liverpool, that 1-1 draw may well have turned into a victory, as that same evening under the floodlights on a mudded Ibrox pitch, Albert engineered a victory for his red-shirted Army team mates.

With seven minutes gone, he had crafted the opening goal for McInnes, scoring a second himself just before half time. Blunstone almost added a third in the second half, again following excellent work from Albert.

There was little doubt that Albert's play in recent weeks had seen him re-capture some of his old form and it was perfect timing with interest in the FA Cup on-going and those two wins and a draw in the First Division easing the problems on that front, edging Wednesday into a much more comfortable mid-table position. But those March winds certainly did blow cold.

Although media attention was a far cry from its modern-day equivalent, Albert Quixall's name was always good for a story and when he was spotted at Arsenal's Highbury stadium as February drew to a close, the rumour mill was up and running and the men of the press began bombarding the north London club with questions, asking if they were in the process of making a bid for the Sheffield Wednesday player.

Albert had indeed been at Highbury on the morning of February 27th, a matter of hours prior to Sheffield Wednesday's match across town at Stamford Bridge. There was, however, nothing untoward in the visit and certainly no talks as to a possible transfer. He was there, explained Wednesday manager Eric Taylor, simply to have some action photographs taken; because of his constant Army duties, he was seldom available for that sort of thing at Hillsborough. So, with Wednesday in London, staying at a hotel close to Highbury, the perfect opportunity arose and permission granted for the photographs to be taken at Arsenal's ground.

The FA Cup sixth round tie, heady heights for Sheffield Wednesday, produced another 'full-house' at Hillsborough for the visit of Bolton Wanderers, and once again the outcome was undecided at the first time of asking with the game finishing a 1-1 draw. Four days later, however, Wembley drew a step closer with an emphatic 2-0 victory in the replay. That dream date below the twin towers, however, was to evaporate on March 27th when Preston North End scored two without reply in the Maine Road semi-final. An injury to Albert just before the interval, with the game still a 0-0 stalemate, hampered his second half performance and some rough-house treatment at the hands of Tommy Docherty, who was spoken to quite severely by the referee and had his boots inspected, didn't help matters.

In the League, the opening March fixture, at home to Blackpool saw a Quixall-less Sheffield Wednesday take the field, as once again, the Army stepped in and denied his release as they wanted him in their line-up to face the Belgian Army in Brussels the following day.

Such matters didn't simply inconvenience Sheffield Wednesday, but also numerous other clubs up and down the country, and why the Army was allowed to dictate if and when players would be released leaves one scratching one's head. It was something akin to a clan chief calling on members of the clan to fight for him whether they wanted to or not.

During his National Service, it is difficult to do a complete statistical review of how many games he actually played. You can trawl through countless newspapers and find Army teams who were scheduled to play on such and such a date, but whether or not those fixtures took place, or if Albert Quixall took part is another investigation altogether. As well as that Rangers fixture in February 1954, games against Billingham Synthonia at Newcastle, and in Plymouth and Exeter are mentioned. If he did play in that trio of fixtures, plus the five League and Cup fixtures, that amounts to eight games in that twenty-eight-day period. Arguably too much.

Sheffield Wednesday's extended cup-run was an exciting time for the club and its supporters, but if anything was to benefit from it, then it was the Wednesday bank balance due to the 237,000 plus who watched the home ties, plus whatever was made from the others.

With a month of the season remaining, Wednesday were five points clear of second bottom Middlesbrough, but those five points also separated nine teams. Three consecutive defeats, against Aston Villa, Huddersfield Town and Portsmouth did little to avert the threat of relegation, something that was becoming part of the end of season expectancy. A 4-2 victory away at Sunderland eased those niggling relegation concerns ever so slightly, but a return to the North East seven days later, and a 3-0 defeat at the hands of Newcastle United nudged them into eighteenth, with two games remaining. Thankfully, a 0-0 draw at home to Wolverhampton Wanderers in the penultimate game of the season saw Wednesday safe.

Albert had only missed one of those final seven fixtures, against Huddersfield Town, due to Army commitments, but had returned to the Wednesday side, eager to play his part in the battle to avoid the drop and duly turned on the style against Portsmouth, with the *Portsmouth Evening News* proclaiming him the outstanding individual on the pitch, whilst adding that *"he also established himself as something of a comedian."* With Portsmouth having been awarded a free kick, he had *'juggled with the ball, and balancing it on his forehead, walked jauntily, if not majestically, to the spot where Dickinson was waiting to take it. And in response to the crowd's good-natured cries of 'Big-ead' he waved his acknowledgement."*

It was ninety-minutes that seemed to see Albert Quixall turn a corner, regain his panache and once again become the player who at one time had promised so much.

Wednesday's inadequacies in the First Division basement area did little to affect Albert's ability and with his, let's say, mediocre performances in the white shirt of his country in the distant past, it came as a shock to many that he was not included amongst the possibles for the full England side and its 'B' side for the forthcoming summer tours at the end of the season. According to the press, some of those whose names appeared on that preliminary list were not and never would be England class; they scratched their heads in wonder at the omission of individuals such as Albert, Stanley Matthews and Duncan Edwards. If excuses were required, it was perhaps Albert's continued National Service, while Edwards, although now a Manchester United first team candidate, was also still of the age to play in their youth team, scheduled to play in a tournament in Switzerland. The trio, however, were also listed to play in the England v Young England fixture at Highbury on the eve of the Cup Final. As things turned out, Albert was later reinstated into the squad, as was Edwards, both to be listed in that of the 'B' team.

Despite his experience, he was still only twenty, it was in the Young England XI that the name 'Quixall' appeared in that pre-Cup Final fixture against England at Highbury and he turned in a performance that was akin to thumbing his nose at the England selectors sitting watching from the stand.

Five minutes prior to the interval, his cross was headed home by Hines, but that was only something of an add-on to his overall performance. Over the course of the ninety minutes, he got through a considerable amount of work, leading by example, scheming and plotting, whilst running the England defenders off their feet. It was Albert Quixall at his best.

If those stiff collared selectors were unmoved by his performance, there were others who were, with a number of the leading European football critics taking in the game. At the end of the ninety minutes, when asked by John Graydon of the *Green 'Un* who they considered to be the most complete player on the pitch. it was expected the names of Stanley Matthews, Len Shackleton or Wilf Mannion would be well to the fore, but the honour went to Albert Quixall.

From London, it was off to Belfast to face Ireland at Windsor Park, where he was to encounter a minor problem prior to the match. Upon arriving in Belfast, he was robbed of his breakfast in the Midland Hotel with excruciating toothache and an SOS went out to a dentist. Following an extraction he was omitted from the team the following day.

How leave from his Army duties was obtained enabling him to participate in the England tour is perhaps down to there being no fixtures to be fulfilled, or people higher up the ladder pulling rank, but it mattered little, he was off to Yugoslavia and Hungary, which would hopefully be followed by an extended European vacation in Switzerland for the World Cup.

His end of season form was the opposite of that of his club, but at international level, he still had to be treated with kid-gloves, far removed as it was from the challenges of the First Division. He still had a considerable number of years remaining in football; there was no rush by either player or country.

Despite the defeats at the hands of the Yugoslavian and Swiss 'B' teams, Albert was regarded as the outstanding player in both fixtures, and was considered to be *"the nearest approach we have in this country to the Continental style of forward for the way he moves the ball about and runs into position.*

"Quixall is a quick-thinking forward and an impressionable one into the bargain. He took careful note of how the Continental people played the game when he was on tour with both his club and the Army and he modelled his style accordingly.

"Unfortunately, there is one defect in Quixall's set up. This is that he not only does not score goals, but he makes little or no effort to do so. It is a rather sad reflection upon so outstanding a player that he has now played in no fewer than 100 First and Second Division games in this country, in addition to representative matches, for only six goals all told."

At the end of May, the FA named twenty-five players to attend World Cup training in London over a two-day period. Albert and his Wednesday teammate, Jackie Sewell, were both named in the side. Only twenty-two would, however, make the final cut and only twenty-four turned up for the start of that two-day training session. The missing man was Albert Quixall, who had just returned from Germany, but was able to join up for day two.

Despite missing day one, Albert did enough in the second session to be selected in the initial seventeen who would travel to Switzerland, but he was never to pull on his boots other than for the training sessions, the inside-forward positions for the games against Belgium, Switzerland and Uruguay going to Ivor Broadis of Newcastle United and Tommy Taylor of Manchester United in the first of the three games and Broadis and Dennis Wilshaw of Wolverhampton Wanderers for the other two.

Albert did, however, earn some applause when, during a training session in Lucerne, he once again performed his 'party trick', flicking the ball up onto his forehead and proceeding to run half the length of the field with it apparently 'glued' there.

Deprived of action in Switzerland, Albert spent much of the close season in action for Hallam Cricket Club in the Yorkshire Council League, where he was a more than capable batsman.

CHAPTER FOUR
RELEGATION AND RESURGENCE

Since their promotion back to the top flight of the English game at the end of the 1951-52 season, Sheffield Wednesday had perhaps, not struggled, but found the going tough, finishing 18th in season 1952-53 and 19th in 1953-54. Numerous clubs, finding themselves in Wednesday's shoes would have cashed in on their prize asset and with the money received bolstered their playing staff with a couple of new additions in the hope that their fortune might change. On the other hand, that prize asset may well have said that enough was enough and fed up with toiling away at the wrong end of the table requested a move to a club where there was a more positive environment. To the credit of both club and player, Sheffield Wednesday never once contemplated selling Albert Quixall and Albert Quixall never contemplated leaving the familiar surroundings of Hillsborough.

If either party thought that the winds of change would be blowing across Hillsborough sometime soon, then they were to be very misguided, as the 1954-55 season got off to the worst possible start, with only one win in the first five fixtures.

A 4-2 defeat at Wolverhampton Wanderers on the opening day was followed two days later by a similar defeat against Manchester United in the first home game of the season. In the return meeting at Old Trafford on September 1st, United again proved to be too strong for Wednesday and won 2-0, with a similar scoreline being repeated against Sunderland at Roker Park three days later. The only victory of those five opening fixtures being sandwiched between the defeats, 6-3 against Aston Villa at home. Goals galore, which was great for those who paid their money at the turnstiles in the hope of entertainment – ten for and fifteen against, but they also wanted to see their team win, something that could not be relied upon if you were a Sheffield Wednesday supporter.

If there was one chink of light, a glimmer of hope for the weeks and months ahead, it was the name 'Quixall' on the score sheet against Aston Villa. It was, however, hoped that this was not his usual solitary contribution coming as early as the third game of the season.

As per normal, Albert's season was a mixture of Sheffield Wednesday and Army fixtures and no sooner had the campaign got underway, a mere two games old, than he was off playing for the Northern Command against South Shields. That jaunt to the North East from his Catterick camp helped in the build-up of his fitness following the summer lay-off and, coupled with a goal in the 3-1 win, gave him an air of renewed confidence for what lay ahead.

Having become known as 'the goalkeeper's friend' due to his lack of goals, two in a matter of days was unheard of, but having scored for the Northern Command in that August 25th fixture, his name was back on the score sheet three days later in the Wednesday 6-3 victory over Aston Villa. "*Shot Shy Quixall On Mark*" was the headline above Derek Dooley's match report in the *Daily Mirror*, while the *London Daily News* mentioned, somewhat tongue in the check, that "*Quixall Nearly Beats A Record*", going on to say that he liked Aston Villa, having scored his only goal of last season against them, while he almost claimed his best-ever feat of scoring twice in a League game, but his goal-bound effort, following his fourth minute opener, was stopped on the line. They were also quick to point out that he had only scored seven goals in ninety-seven League games!

It had been a long time coming, but that goal against Aston Villa was no ordinary strike, but one fit for the occasion. Picking up a pass from Finney in the middle of the pitch, he veered slightly to the left before hitting the ball from twenty-five yards, giving Parsons in the Villa goal no chance. A goal that pleased player and crowd alike.

Albert was inspirational in that 6-3 victory, but the momentum could not be carried on in the two games that followed against Manchester United and Sunderland, the second of which saw him twist his ankle in what was only the third minute, leaving him as little more than a passenger, hobbling on the wing, for the remainder of the game. Continuing to play through the pain did him no good whatsoever and he was to miss the next three fixtures.

Wednesday's results during his three-game absence were mixed, with a win, a draw and a defeat and, upon returning against Sheffield United on September 18th, he could do little to prevent the solitary goal defeat. Another reversal, against Portsmouth the following Saturday, in which Albert scored in the 2-1 defeat, plunged Wednesday into second bottom spot, level on points with neighbours United.

Since his meteoric rise to fame there had been praise and criticism in more or less equal amounts and it wasn't simply from the man on the terrace that the brickbats or bouquets came. Writing in his regular column in the *Manchester Evening News*, Manchester City's centre-forward Don Revie wrote, in an article preceded by the headline "*Experience, confidence and wisdom count so... Soccer Aces Reach Their Peak Between 25 and 30*" – "*As an example of a young player springing to prominence early, Albert Quixall comes easily to mind. Albert is already recognised throughout the country as a top class inside forward.*

"*But while conceding his exceptional ability I would suggest that in four years' time he will have added to his play a quality which because of his youth is at present dormant.*

"*It is then we may see Quixall as a great player, the finished forward we may well be proud of.*"

We are certainly not going to fast forward those four years as Don Revie mentions, but as you most probably are already aware of the Albert Quixall story, the Manchester City and England man knew what he was talking about, or else, had a crystal ball amongst his playing kit.

If scoring twice in one season was something of a rarity for Albert Quixall, then to score twice in successive fixtures could only give him the confidence and the belief that he could, without a shadow of doubt, add goal scoring to his wide array of talents.

"*Boy Quixall Shoots Up Blackpool*" was the headline on the front page of the *Green 'Un* on Saturday October 2nd, following Wednesday's first win in five games. Coming six minutes from time, it was more than welcome.

He failed to make it three in a row three days later in Glasgow, as Rangers defeated his Army side 3-0 at Ibrox.

As the darker nights drew in and autumn turned to winter, the skies over Hillsborough were equally dark, if not more so than at the other twenty clubs in the First Division, and Sheffield Wednesday fell like the leaves from the trees, as they failed to register a solitary win between October 23rd and March 19th. Twenty-second place in the First Division table became their permanent home.

The defence leaked goals like a sieve. Six against Preston North End, followed by four against Manchester City, then five against Cardiff City. Once into the New Year, there was even a seven against Tottenham Hotspur!

If Albert needed an escape from the often soul-destroying ninety minutes of First Division football, then it came from his Army and other representative fixtures, but these too would often offer up little in the way of relief or a refreshing change. Perhaps he would have benefitted more from a rest, rather than having to play two, sometimes three, games a week. November alone saw him turn out for the Army against an FA XI, Everton and the Belgian Army, while early December took him to London, and Arsenal's Highbury stadium, to face Ireland.

There was, however, the possibility that things could change for the better as his heavy playing schedule was slowly drawing to a close, with January 1955 to see his final game in an Army team, turning out against Scotland at Ibrox. That fixture on January 18th was to be his seventy-ninth of the season – nineteen for Sheffield Wednesday and an incredible sixty for the Army. There could well have been eighty all told and sixty-one for the Army, but boils on his leg rendered him unfit to face the French Army at the end of the month.

Although they say that a change is as good as a rest, even that didn't help, as a switch to right-half from his usual inside-forward role did nothing to alter matters as the decline in Wednesday's fortune continued.

The change in Albert's performances, be it a half back or inside forward, were noticeable to all. Manchester United's Roger Byrne writing in his weekly column for the local *Evening News* mentioned that Albert *"seemed to have lost a lot of his confidence, but it could be argued that when your team, as a whole, are not performing well, it needs more than one individual to drag them out of that hole and get back on winning ways."* Despite his age, and with more seasoned professional around him, Albert carried the weight on his shoulders and against Burnley on March 12th he was said to be outstanding despite Wednesday's 2-0 defeat.

Thankfully, Albert had other things to keep him occupied and forget about football, as he was now engaged, and spending time with his fiancée Jeannette Dunstan was the ideal escape route. It was also to take him down a completely different road, as Jeannette ran a dance studio and she would often put Albert through his pas seul, glissades and entrechats. *"I am just doing it for fun,"* he was to say, *"but if it makes me a better player, I'll be pleased."*

He should have perhaps also taken his teammates along, as Wednesday's season disintegrated around them, the 2-0 victory over Preston North End on March 19th was their first in the League since October 16th. The FA Cup third round victory against Hastings Town, meant nothing, as defeat, in a replay in the next round against Notts County failed to bring a glimmer of light.

A goal against Arsenal on February 26th and another against Bolton Wanderers on April 8th gave Albert five for the season, his best total yet, while Wednesday somehow managed to win three of their last four games, the last of the quartet, a 5-0 victory over West Bromwich Albion. Too little, too late, as relegation had long been on the cards.

Despite his overall performances, coupled with that of Sheffield Wednesday, it came as something of a surprise that he was included in the England squad for a trio of friendly fixtures at the end of May and, although missing from the line-up that faced France in the first of the three, he played against Spain and came on as substitute for Nat Lofthouse against Portugal.

Coming on to replace Lofthouse in the 39th minute, it is difficult to believe that this would be his final appearance in the white shirt of England at the tender age of twenty-one, more so considering that the average age of the team that faced the Portuguese was around twenty-eight, only lessened by the inclusion of eighteen-year-old Duncan Edwards, while Stanley Matthews was over forty!

Following such a dismal season League-wise, it would not have come as a surprise if Albert had called time on his Sheffield Wednesday career and asked for transfer. Perhaps if he had been aware of the fact that his England career was at a premature end, then that transfer request would have been placed on Eric Taylor's desk. But he was a Sheffield boy, a life-long Wednesday supporter and back in those post-war days, loyalty meant a lot. Wages within the game were basically the same wherever you went, with a maximum wage of £15 per week. Yes, there were tales of brown envelopes changing hands, or being left on kitchen tables after a player had agreed a move to another club, but it would not have mattered whether he was playing for Wednesday or Arsenal, his pay packet would have been the same weight. Only on field results might have been different.

Perhaps due to Sheffield Wednesday's relegation, Albert felt that he owed the club something. Perhaps he was saddened that his team were now a Second Division side and he wanted to rectify matters and get them back into the top flight where he believed they belonged. But it wasn't simply a case of getting them back, but helping them prolong that stay and attempting to establish them as one of the top sides in the country. A huge task, considering the quickly developing Manchester United under Matt Busby, with its incomparable youth system and the strong Wolverhampton Wanderers side under the leadership of England captain Billy Wright.

No matter what, Albert Quixall remained a Sheffield Wednesday player and prepared himself for another sojourn in the Second Division of the Football League for the 1955-56 season.

The Second Division of 1955 comprised of something of a mixed bunch, containing the likes of Bury, Notts County and Lincoln City on one hand, with Liverpool and Leicester City on the other. But no matter who the opposition were, the games had to be won if promotion was to be achieved, and if any inspiration was required it came twofold on Saturday August 20th as the season got underway with a bang. Not only did Wednesday open their campaign with a victory, 5-2 against Plymouth Argyle, the name Quixall appeared twice on the scoresheet. His first, ten minutes into the second half, had given Wednesday a 2-1 advantage, while his second of the afternoon, in the final minute of the game, emphasised Wednesday's superiority.

Overshadowed by a Sewell hat-trick, it mattered little, as both club and player were off the mark and things could only get better. Results-wise it could have been better, spoilt by seven draws between mid-August and the beginning of October, coupled with one defeat, whilst there were no more Quixall goals.

The trial as a half back was forgotten and it was back to his inside-forward role and following the 4-0 victory over Bristol Rovers at the beginning of September he was considered as being back to his best. *"After the interval the Wednesday came right into their own with 'pure' football played by craftsmen, and, there was a dazzling exhibition by young Albert Quixall,"* wrote a correspondent for the *Bristol Evening Post*, adding: *"Quixall, in the language of the Soccer profession, played a 'blinder.' Now that he is out of the Army and receiving the benefit of full-time training he should develop into a really great player, and I use the word great advisedly."*

Although, a week later, another reporter who frequented the press box on behalf of the *Lincolnshire Echo* considered Albert to be disappointing and said *"he was quiet – so quiet indeed that he successfully lost himself.*" It could be considered little more than sour grapes as Albert had engineered his side's second goal of the afternoon in the 2-2 draw.

A goal in another 2-2 draw, this time against Hull City towards the end of October, was followed by the only goal of the game against Port Vale – "*Quixall Goal Pierces Iron Curtain*" and one in the 3-3 draw with Bury, as October drew to a close. But despite having suffered only two defeats in thirteen fixtures, that top spot in the Second Division had still not been claimed.

As November reared its head, there was something of a role reversal for Albert, as despite now languishing in the Second Division, he had not been forgotten and found himself selected for an FA XI to face the Army at St James' Park, Newcastle, giving a good account of himself in the 2-2 draw. But he continued to be something of an enigma for members of the press. *"If Quixall's sense of urgency had matched his love of the artistic, Wednesday might have won even more easily. It is a great pity that Quixall so seldom makes 100 per cent use of his great gifts,"* appeared in the *Yorkshire Post and Leeds Intelligencer* following the 3-0 victory over Barnsley.

It had now been almost four years since his League debut and something of an infinite number of games, plus that handful of England caps, but still a huge question mark hovered alongside his name, whilst having been lauded and lambasted in equal amounts. That he had the talent had never been up for debate and had those games been matched with goals, then he would undoubtedly have been the best thing since sliced bread, but even forgetting about those goals, there was still some missing ingredient. Had Sheffield Wednesday been able to cultivate the Quixall/Dooley partnership, there is no telling how things would have worked out for the club and those individuals, but without doubt it was the shortage of goals that had led to Wednesday's downfall and perhaps also that of Albert Quixall.

Christmas Eve and a 4-0 victory over Stoke City, Albert claiming the fourth, gave everyone around Hillsborough an early Christmas present in the form of leadership of the Second Division for the first time that season and they were there to stay for the remainder of the campaign. There was a new-found confidence around the place, and in Albert Quixall, who now had his shooting boots as, along with his Wednesday team mates, had the newest low-cut style, made in Germany.

It was no idle boast, as the strike against Stoke was followed by nine in eleven games, with a further two thrown in for good measure by the end of the season. Seventeen in thirty-nine games was certainly a more favourable total than anything in the past.

Although there wasn't a goal beside his name, there was, however, an excellent ninety minutes for Young England against their Scottish counterparts at Hillsborough, creating a goal for Johnny Haynes, forcing the Scottish goalkeeper Morrison to make four brilliant saves and see another effort cleared off the line. Despite that, there was no place for him in the England 'B' side to face Switzerland in March.

Strangely, that influx of goals, coupled with notable performances, had coincided with a change in his personal circumstances in February 1956, when he got married to his fiancée Jeanette Dunstan at Wardsley Parish Church on Monday March 5th. A double celebration would have been the ideal wedding present (although his new wife was not much of a football fan), but it wasn't until April 26th and the penultimate game of the season against Bury away, that the Second Division championship was guaranteed.

The 4-0 victory over Stoke City on Christmas Eve had kick-started the race towards the eventual championship, as it was followed by a draw, win, loss, win, loss sequence, before six victories, with another defeat sandwiched in between setting the pace, giving Wednesday a four-point advantage over Leicester City, with Liverpool a further point behind.

A look at the Second Division table following the 2-1 victory over Leicester City on Easter Monday painted a completely different picture, as Leicester were now eight points adrift in sixth, level on points with Liverpool. Wednesday's nearest challengers were now Bristol Rovers, Blackburn Rovers and Port Vale, six and seven points behind respectively. There seemed to be little danger of Wednesday being caught, but a 3-3 draw at West Ham United, followed by a 3-2 defeat at home to Fulham saw Bristol Rovers narrow the gap to three points, with Leeds United now in third place, a further point behind, with two games remaining.

By a strange quirk of fate, Leeds United played host to Bristol Rovers the following Saturday, so something had to give, and while Wednesday were hammering home five against Bury, their Yorkshire neighbours defeated Bristol Rovers by the odd goal in three. The championship was secured.

Goals had been the problem in the past. The 1953-54 campaign saw only Woodhead, Sewell and Shaw hit double figures, scoring fifty-seven of Wednesday's seventy goals between them. The following season, 54-55, was worse: Sewell's fourteen and Shaw's ten the only double figures. The 1955-56 season, however, was rounded off with another quintet of goals on the final day against Lincoln City, with Sewell, Froggatt,

Broadbent, Shiner and a certain Albert Quixall, all hitting double figures. Albert's goal in that 5-2 championship-deciding ninety minutes against Bury was his seventeenth of the season.

Offering his opinion prior to the Bury fixture, as to why things had changed for the Wednesday inside forward, Fred Walters of the *Green 'Un* wrote: *"I am prepared for him to be named for both the game against Brazil and for the FA's Continental tour. Wednesday follower's will attribute this to his readiness this season to have a crack at goal. When all's said and done. 16 goals in 37 appearances are far more convincing than his mere 13 in all his earlier appearances put together when he averaged about one goal per 10 or 11 games.*

"He has got over that phase when the theorists encouraged him to play "deep," for, truth to tell, I doubt whether there are many forwards in the game who really understand anything about the "deep" game.

"Football is a simple game and there is nothing to beat it being played in a simple straight forward manner.

"British football has paid dearly for all the post-war theories which have left so many people utterly 'stone cold.' "

An international re-call was still very much on the cards, with an appearance in the Football League side to face the League of Ireland offering him something of a stepping stone, although the subsequent 5-2 defeat did little to enhance the possibilities. But with England scheduled to play four friendlies in May, against Brazil at Wembley and against Sweden, Finland and West Germany on a short tour, the opportunity was there and, although his season had been played out in the Second

Division, he had finally produced goals alongside the flair and many expected his return to the full England set up to be guaranteed. They, like Albert, were to be left disappointed and mystified as his name was missing from the squad.

He did, however, get to face the Brazilians, but it was not the international eleven, but club side Vasco Da Gama, who did have five internationals in their side, in the Olympic Stadium, Amsterdam in a friendly in aid of the Dutch War Charities. Unlike England who won their fixture 4-2, Wednesday went down to a 2-0 defeat in an end of season friendly.

In the eyes of many, the forthcoming 1956-57 season was not just make or break for Sheffield Wednesday, but also for Albert Quixall. The Hillsborough club couldn't continue on its yo-yoing existence, plunging from the First Division to the Second before bouncing back again, only to see the process repeated with much unwanted regularity. From Albert Quixall's perspective, he had left the mantle of "promising youngster" behind and was now an experienced professional. With Wednesday, it was no problem maintaining his first team place, but his status as an England player had diminished and others were now breaking through, leaving his opportunities limited. There was also a World Cup a couple of years down the line and having missed out when it came to places in the squad for the 1954 tournament, there was the added target of making the cut for Sweden in 1958.

The 1956-57 season, from the perspective of both club and player, could not have got off to a better start, with three victories in the opening four fixtures: 4-2 at home to West Bromwich Albion, 4-0, also at home, against Chelsea, a 3-1 loss at Portsmouth and a 4-0 triumph over Newcastle United. Forgetting that defeat down on the south coast, it was a more than favourable start to the campaign with not just Sheffield Wednesday getting off the starting blocks with some momentum, but also four goals from Albert Quixall, one each against West Bromwich and Newcastle and a double against Chelsea.

Albert signalled his intentions for the season ahead within five minutes of that first whistle being blown against West Bromwich Albion, when he saw a goal-bound effort rebound off the foot of the post with the keeper beaten. He was to become a thorn in the Albion side over the rest of the ninety-minutes, scoring Wednesday's third, coming close to increasing his total on other occasions, whilst prompting his fellow team mates.

"The most accomplished player on the field and must soon come back into England reckoning" – Birmingham Daily Gazette.

Although only ninety minutes old, it had been an ideal start to the season and, along with his four goals in the three games that followed, he had re-kindled the interest of not only the influential members of the press, but that of the England selectors. Although Wednesday's momentum faltered, losing to Cardiff City and drawing with Charlton Athletic, Albert continued to make his presence felt, making him difficult to ignore.

"*Selectors Hear Quixall's Call*" shouted George Follows in the *Daily Herald* following the 4-4 draw against Charlton Athletic: *"A voice rang through the Valley on Saturday calling 'Roy.' Twenty-one thousand Charlton fans heard it… England team-manager Walter Winterbottom heard it… Albert Quixall, of Sheffield Wednesday, was shouting himself back into international football.*

"The ball was still on its way to Quixall when he shouted to centre-forward Roy Shiner that he was going to give him a goal. A goal it was…. the best of eight equally shared by both sides. Mr Winterbottom was visibly impressed by this quick appreciation of Soccer situations."

So, for many, it came as no surprise when "Albert Quixall (Sheffield Wednesday)" appeared amongst the names for the Football League to face the League of Ireland on September 19th 1956 in Dublin. *"Boy with the bikini shorts gets another chance of establishing himself as the new Wilf Mannion. He steps into the league side at inside right to form a partnership with Johnny Haynes that should restore memories of the palmy days of Mannion and Raich Carter"* wrote Dennis Shaw in the *Birmingham Daily Gazette*. He continued: *"Quixall for Dennis Wilshaw is the only change from the England team which conjured up World Cup dreams by defeating Germany 3-1 in Berlin last May. The recall of young Quixall, who along with Haynes is one of the best youngsters in the game in a pure footballing sense, will be popular in most quarters for there has been an outcry for his return to the England side since the season opened. Since his demobilisation from the Army, the stocky, blond haired inside man has matured considerably having developed a flair for the opening which should result in a lucrative partnership with Haynes. Quixall won the first of his five England caps in October, 1953, when he was a member of the side which beat Wales 4-1 at Cardiff with Wilshaw at inside left. Wilshaw is, of course, not considered now since he is playing in the Wolves' reserve side awaiting a transfer."*

It was praise laced with unnecessary and certainly unwanted pressure, as once again there was the comparison with Wilf Mannion, an individual from a different era who would undoubtedly have achieved more had it not been for the Second World War. Would Albert Quixall never be rid of the comparison and allowed to be his own man?

This was something also raised by Jack Peart in the *Sunday Mirror* of September 16th: *"Praise is heady wine for any youngster trembling on the brink of sporting fame.*

"*A few lucky lads can taste it, savour it and still remain unspoilt. Others gulp it down and become intoxicated with their own importance until they really see themselves as others see them!*

"*Nobody should know that better than Albert Quixall, Sheffield Wednesday's 'Golden Boy' at last fulfilling the promise he showed four years ago.*

"*Quixall is a typical example of the crazy, talent starved, business-bedevilled, post-war Soccer set-up.*

"*Potentially great young players like Albert are exploited and lionised as blatantly as film companies boost their top-heavy charmers for box-office benefits.*

"*With his obvious football ability, baby face, unruly mop of fair hair and abbreviated shorts, Quixall was a 'natural' for the big build-up.*

"*He was lauded to the skies.*

"*Stan Cullis, Wolves manager, called him 'undoubtedly one of the great players of the future.'*

"*Quixall was literally written into the England international team long before his natural talents could develop.*

"*It was hardly surprising therefore that he never lived up to the promise of 'another Wilf Mannion' as he was so often, and so unfairly described.*

"*At the time, I warned 'Pic' readers that Quixall was being press ganged into international football long before he was ready.*

"*You can't blame youngsters like Quixall for believing they are better, than they really are – or for thinking that they know it all.*

"*One bad game can erase the pleasant memories of a dozen 'blinders' and Albert Quixall discovered this the hard way.*

"*It wasn't long before the very critics who had praised him so lavishly were lambasting him for failing to live up to their own superlatives.*

"*And so, it seemed that at the ripe old age of 21, Albert boasted the distinction of being an 'ex-international.'*

"*It taught Quixall something.*

"*He changed his style from goal-maker to goal scorer and now he's back again with a great chance of winning a permanent place in the new young England team."*

It was certainly no low-key return to the international stage in Dublin as every newspaper was to mention that "*Quixall will be anxious to impress,*" but Albert simply shut his ears and eyes to the overflowing column inches and concentrated on the ninety minutes that lay ahead. A somewhat strange encounter that was not viewed favourably by the men in the press box.

Thankfully, however, Albert was to escape their wrath, scoring a ninth minute equaliser after the Irish had stunned their opponents sixty seconds previously to take the lead. By half time, it was 3-1 to the visitors, but their hosts fought back to clinch a draw. He was considered to be only one of three Football League players to emerge with credit.

The England selectors, however, were not of a similar mind and he was not selected for the match against Northern Ireland at Windsor Park, Belfast on October 6th. They did include Stanley Matthews, at the age of 41 and 248 days, in what was considered to be a disappointing ninety minutes. Matthews scored in the second minute, Ireland equalising four minutes from time. Edgar Turner, in the *Sunday Mirror* wrote, following the match that he would *"play the whole Manchester United team, with Albert Quixall in for Billy Whelan. Alternatively, put Quixall in as a quick-striker alongside Tommy Taylor."*

A 3-2 victory over Sunderland at Hillsborough on October 6th and a 4-1 triumph over Tottenham Hotspur on November 17th, again on home soil, were the only bright spots of a dismal eight-week period when all the other fixtures ended in defeat, a dismal time around the steel city and a period that well and truly snookered Albert Quixall's hopes of returning to the England set up. Had he scored a couple of goals or more during that time, then things might have been different, with inclusion in the side to face Wales on November 14th and Yugoslavia fourteen days later.

The white number eight shirt on both occasions was given to Johnny Brooks of Tottenham, who was to score on his debut against the Welsh, making him an instant hero, leaving the selectors with a smug smile on their faces. But when Brooks and Albert came head-to-head in the League fixture sandwiched in between those two internationals, there was only one winner.

Even the London based newspapers couldn't deny that Albert was the better of the pair. *"It seemed difficult to understand how Brooks earned his England cap. He was played right out of the picture by Quixall,"* appeared in the *Weekly Despatch*.

If there was any form of compensation then it came with the announcement that he had been named among the twenty-two players for the forthcoming World Cup qualifiers against Denmark.

His selection, coupled with the performance in the ninety minutes against Tottenham brought a spring back to his step. There were also further goals to his credit: one against Tottenham, followed by a double in the 2-1 defeat of Aston Villa, in an exquisite performance, and another in the 4-1 win over West Bromwich Albion. You could also throw in another double in the historic Sheffield v Glasgow inter-city fixture. The *Liverpool Daily Post* considered him a *"reformed character in that he played much less theatrically than of old,"* in Wednesday's 1-0 defeat against Everton at Goodison Park.

Like the London-based newspapers, following the 4-1 Tottenham victory, the Birmingham based dailies waxed in a similar fashion following his performance in the 2-1 victory over Aston Villa on December 1st. *"In Sheffield, a chubby-faced young footballer, Albert Quixall, gets the hero worship normally accorded only to the Johnny Rays and Frankie Vaughans of this world, and if his performance against Aston Villa at Hillsborough on Saturday is any guide, such adulation is hardly misplaced.*

"No doubt inspired by the possibility that a bright display might see him back in the England team again – his is among the 22 names put forward for the coming World Cup matches – this rumbustious young man played such ducks and drakes with Villa's normally sound defence that the Wednesday should have won by a much more comfortable margin than two goals to one."

There was, however, no place in the England eleven to face Denmark at Molineux, and the 5-2 victory certainly didn't disprove the selectors' decision, although it was the Manchester United pairing of Tommy Taylor and Duncan Edwards who were to share the five goals between them, the former with a hat trick and the latter forsaking his normal half-back position for that of inside left. With Manchester United currently ruling the roost in the English game, one wonders how the career of Albert Quixall could have unfolded, playing in a team full of confidence, which was growing with every passing ninety minutes.

1957 began brightly, although his trio of goals in the FA Cup against Preston North End failed to take Sheffield Wednesday into the Fourth Round. The first game was a 0-0 stalemate, he scored once in the 2-2 draw of the replay, and notched his team's only goal in the 5-1 second replay thrashing. In the First Division, he found the net in the 2-1 win over leaders Manchester United and another in the 6-3 defeat at the hands of Arsenal. February was equally promising, with goals against Sunderland and Manchester City, although neither were match winners, nor contributed to victories, and Wednesday remained in 16th place.

With her husband grabbing the headlines on a seemingly regular basis, something that he had done since his schoolboy days, Jeanette Quixall was more than content to remain in the background. She was, however, thrust into the spotlight, like it or not, for a 'Meet The Family' feature that was to appear in the *South Shields Football Gazette*. Alongside a photograph of the couple *"selecting a record for their radiogram,"* appeared the following: *"Although before her marriage, Mrs. Jeanette Quixall, wife of Albert Quixall, the Sheffield Wednesday and English international inside forward, made her living as a teacher of ballet, she also had an interest in the more conventional types of dancing, and actually met her husband at a dance in Sheffield.*

"It was perhaps fitting that the young couple should meet each other in such a way, or in addition to his wife's talents in that direction, Quixall himself is noted for his brilliant footwork on the football field.

"As well as teaching, Jeanette ran her own ballet school for five years prior to her marriage, though she subsequently gave it up in order to devote her full-time attention to looking after the home which she and Albert have set up in a house owned by the Sheffield Wednesday club.

"Albert and his wife have no particular methods of spending their leisure hours, preferring instead to have as much time as they possibly can in each other's company, but readers will probably have heard of the birth of a son to the young couple – a fortnight ago – and the name favoured at the moment for the new arrival is Paul."

With two months of the 1956-57 season remaining, Sheffield Wednesday were five points off the second bottom place Portsmouth in the First Division, with Charlton Athletic presenting little concern, propping everyone else up, a further five points adrift. Although there were still a dozen games remaining, the general opinion was that Sheffield Wednesday were safe from relegation. But those alarm bells rang when the five March fixtures produced only one victory, one draw and three defeats, pushing then down a couple of places to eighteenth. There was, however, still a five-point gap between them and second bottom.

Matters could certainly have been a lot worse had it not been for Albert's contribution with the winning goal in that solitary victory over Wolverhampton Wanderers on March 9th, while he was also to find the net in 3-2 home defeat at the hands of Leeds United.

But it was in the final seven April fixtures that the Hillsborough faithful were to be more than grateful for the 'new, all-singing, all-dancing, goal-scoring' Albert Quixall. His penalty secured a point in the 2-2 home draw with Everton, another penalty secured a 3-0 victory over Luton Town, also at home, while a double penalty strike ensured yet another home victory against Preston North End. Twenty-two goals from forty-one League outings were a more than favourable return for the inside forward who couldn't score.

It is difficult to fathom out how such a change had occurred in Albert Quixall's overall play. In years gone by, he had the skill and the technique, which went without question; it was simply the goals that were missing from his make-up. Did he possess an inborn fear of shooting, simply believing that his forte as an inside forward was as a goal-maker and that the scoring was for others? Perhaps if Derek Dooley and Jackie Sewell had not been around and so dependable when it came to scoring, then he might have taken on more of the responsibility. Perhaps, as mentioned previously, it was Sheffield Wednesday's style of play, keeping him at arm's length from the front line.

However, the main reason may well have been nothing more than having been so talented, he was pushed into the spotlight too early, more so with England than with Sheffield Wednesday and he ultimately paid the price.

On the international scene, he remained a possibility and was named amongst the twenty-two players for the forthcoming fixtures against Ireland and Denmark in May, but that was simply it, named in the squad, nothing more, the inside-right position going to Bristol City's John Atyeo. It reflected on how far Albert's international star had fallen from the sky, that, although many tipped him for an England return, it was a Second Division player that kept him out of the team. But to be fair to Atyeo, he grabbed his fourth England appearance against the Republic of Ireland at Wembley on May 8th with both hands, scoring twice in the 5-1 victory, once in 4-1 win over Denmark a week later, followed by another goal in the return fixture against the Republic of Ireland on May 19th, but somewhat ironically, never appeared in a white jersey again.

CHAPTER FIVE
ENOUGH IS ENOUGH

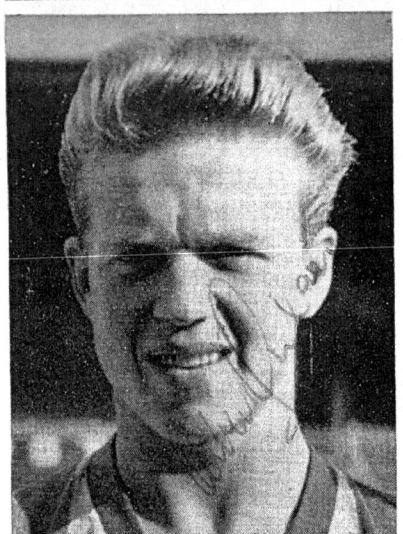

ALBERT QUIXALL (Sheffield Wed.)

Sheffield Wednesday's 1957-58 season faced something of a knock-out blow even before the first whistle had been blown, with the cancellation of their proposed opener against Manchester City at Maine Road on August 24th due to the team being decimated by flu, with only six of their twenty-six players in training, leaving them unable to fulfil the fixture. Things failed to improve, with the second match of the season against Newcastle United, the following Wednesday, also being called off. Such was the seriousness of the epidemic that the club doctor was forced to shut the ground.

Somehow, reporters from the *Daily Herald* and the *Daily Mirror* managed to contact Albert who was reported to have '*croaked*:' *"I feel worse... my back is causing me more trouble. I feel as if my back is breaking. When I woke this morning, I could hardly move."* What was equally disappointing to Albert, besides missing the start of the season, immediately putting Wednesday on the back foot, was having to miss the Northern Professionals Golf Championship at Leeds.

"I am keeping my fingers crossed so that I don't catch Albert's flu," said his wife Jeanette, *"it would be very awkward with a young baby in the house."*

Mystery had always surrounded Albert Quixall and England, the 'was he too young', 'should he have played instead of such and such', or whatever other questions arose, left one to wonder what the real reasons were behind his non-appearances, as he was to appear in a series of newspaper articles entitled 'Educated Soccer' by England team manager, and also the Football Association coaching director Walter Winterbottom.

With international selection having been the employ of "the dim bland men," some of whom might never even have kicked a ball in earnest, there was always going to be the debate that they were biased against certain individuals, for reasons known only to themselves. In Albert's case, perhaps he was seen as something of a young upstart, an individual who ruffled the feathers of the starched collared, strict, set-in-their-ways selectors from a completely different generation.

Nevertheless, he did have his admirers and featured in that aforementioned series, part of three new FA film strips, which were available to clubs and schools, picked out various techniques, such as passing, the use of the instep, with images of Albert demonstrating what was what. Strange, using a player who was no longer part of the set up, but it can only be imagined that the filming was done whilst he still was; even so, it must have been quite a while before.

August 31st finally saw Sheffield Wednesday's season get out of the starting blocks, but, by the third fixture, they were already second bottom, albeit having played two games less than their rivals, but the warning signs were already there, with one win and two defeats in that opening trio of fixtures.

Being back on familiar territory at the foot of the First Division was to be only of minor concern around Hillsborough. What was more troubling were the headlines following the 2-1 defeat at home to West Bromwich Albion on September 14th – not those being critical of yet another inept Wednesday performance – but: *"Newcastle Will Bid For Quixall"* in *The People*. *"Newcastle United are back in business! And the man they want is 23-year-old Albert Quixall, Sheffield Wednesday's international inside right.*

"Expect Newcastle chief Stan Seymour to move in with a firm offer within the next few days. He certainly means to land a new international inside forward, despite the failure to lure Celtic's Willie Fernie.

"Recently, Newcastle suggested an exchange deal involving their Scottish centre half Bill Paterson for a Glasgow Rangers' forward but there was nothing doing.

"Now you can take it from us, Quixall is the player they hope to get."

That report didn't simply cause waves, it started a tsunami as the *Daily Mirror* of the following day carried the headline: *"Quixall In Showdown"*, with Archie Ledbrooke writing: *"It looks as though a League club is trying to 'steal' Albert Quixall.*

"Sheffield Wednesday secretary-manager Eric Taylor dramatically told me of this yesterday, and also brought into the open trouble which has been brewing for some days between Wednesday and their England international inside forward.

"Alleging that another club had been trying to 'tap' Quixall, manager Taylor told me. "After our game at Portsmouth last Saturday week, I called in Quixall as part of the match inquest. He told me he was not happy.

"I told him I wasn't happy either, because we were not winning matches. And I instructed him to come back and see me in another week.

"He could give me no reason why he should not be happy. All his relatives and friends live within two or three miles, and so do those of his wife.

"He has had a £750 benefit and in two years he will be entitled to a second benefit of £1,000. He has had from us absolutely everything he is entitled to.'

"Quixall, five times capped for England, has not asked for a transfer. On that report Taylor said: 'I think this is a calculated leak by another club. That is why I think they are trying to approach him.'

"What other club? The Wednesday manager answered: 'We hadn't better talk about that.'

"He added: 'But if it goes before my directors and they decide he shall go, we would want a bigger fee for him than we paid for Jackie Sewell.'

"All Quixall would say yesterday was: 'I think a move would do my football good. I think I could better myself. But it is not true that I have been approached by another club.

'Sheffield Wednesday are a good club, but I think a change would be in the interests of everybody.' "

Coming completely out of the blue, the decision to ask for a transfer could only hint that an illegal approach had been made. Why now? The situation regarding club and country had not changed; yes, he was now scoring goals on a regular basis, boosting his CV and making himself more attractive to other clubs, but, now happily married with a young family, the promise of some extra cash would not have been unwelcome.

Somewhat ironically, a couple of days after the news of Newcastle's interest in the player and Albert's interest in a move, the *Daily Mirror* carried an article on 'fiddling.' The Football League was planning to introduce new measures to prevent clubs from offering "*furs and diamonds for player's wives and a new car 'gift' for the players*," aiming to stamp out "*the under the counter smear, and stopping the 'spiv' deals to reward players*." Their proposal was to introduce a maximum basic wage of £1,040 a year (£20 per week) for all players after their seventeenth birthday and a 2½ per cent cut of transfer fees for players in addition to the present accrued share of benefit.

There was even talk of installing 'financial detectives' in various big towns who would be given the power to make spot checks on the books of any club suspected of continuing under the counter deals. A new 'get tough' rule would also be installed which would allow the Football League to expel clubs found guilty of making illegal payments in cash or in kind to players, their relatives or friends when they moved.

But by the time such rules and relegations were implemented, who knows what shady deals might have taken place?

Sheffield Wednesday were quick to deny the reports that suggested Albert had asked for a transfer, with manager Eric Taylor saying that should he eventually decide to ask for a move then he would recommend the directors not to accept it. *"Wednesday simply cannot afford to let him go. There isn't enough money in football to buy Albert."* He was also to reveal that when Albert was doing his National Service at Catterick, he was approached by another club who were interested in signing him.

No matter what, the die had been cast, even although the chat between manager and player had ended with a shake of hands and the announcement that Albert was to remain a Sheffield Wednesday player. What was said behind the closed door of the manager's office at Hillsborough was not recorded, but it could be suggested that a couple of pointers were made to money, that made Albert reconsider, or perhaps outweighed any thoughts of moving.

Having just received his due £750 benefit, with the second of £1,000 on the distant horizon, had he moved, then his next payment would only have been £750. He would have been a financial loser.

A loser he might well have been, but Sheffield Wednesday would have been the biggest losers, as, having shrugged off the transfer debacle, he got his head down and soon resumed his goal-scoring performances from the tail end of the previous season.

In the two fixtures following the breaking interest from Newcastle United, Wednesday lost further ground with a 4-1 defeat at Leicester City and a 4-2 defeat at Tottenham Hotspur, plunging them to the foot of the table. A goal-less draw against the would-be Quixall suitors, Newcastle, and a 5-3 victory over Birmingham City, with Albert scoring twice, eased the problem slightly, but four consecutive defeats, without a goal being scored in earnest, quickly returned them to that 22nd place in the First Division, level on points with fellow strugglers Leicester City.

A goal in the 3-3 draw with Sunderland, another in the 5-4 defeat at Bolton Wanderers and a penalty in the 2-0 victory over Arsenal, in a draw, lose, win, lose, win sequence failed to improve matters much as October blended into November.

With Wednesday's on-going First Division problems, coupled with his rather indifferent start to the season, the England selectors showed little interest in him, but he was given the opportunity to push for a place in forthcoming fixtures when a Yorkshire select side met the England 'B' side to commemorate the centenary of Sheffield F.C., the oldest of all football clubs.

Under the spotlight, as ever, Albert didn't disappoint the 25,000, whilst giving the watching selectors something to think about, scoring once, making two others and coming close on other occasions, in an excellent performance, contained within a thrilling nine goal encounter that England 'B' won 5-4.

Perhaps those selectors should have paid more attention to Irish international Danny Blanchflower who suggested that they should select more players who are playing well in bad sides!

A place on the bench for the Football League's visit to Belfast to face the Irish League should have been a welcome change of scenery, but it was to be scuppered by a thigh injury, which also forced him to miss four games. His contribution when not in the Wednesday line-up was always missed, as were his goals, but neither could do anything to prevent Wednesday's prolonged stay at the foot of the First Division.

The FA Cup brought a much-needed break from the rigours and disappointments of the First Division against lower league opposition. Although on Wednesday's current form, anyone would have fancied their chances of beating them, they managed to dispose of Hereford United (3-0) and Hull City (4-3), setting up a plum tie with Manchester United at Old Trafford on February 15th.

It was the afternoon of Thursday February 6th. The football world was stunned by the news that the plane bringing the Manchester United team and officials back to Britain after playing Red Star Belgrade in a European Cup tie had crashed upon take-off, after a re-fuelling stop in Munich.

"I was at home in Warley Road, Sheffield, listening to the radio when this news flash came on about the crash", recalled Albert. *"Immediately, my first thoughts were, what the hell is going to happen to the match the following week, little realising the gravity of the situation. Naturally when the grim news came through about the players, it left me very sad indeed. You see, these were great pals of mine, from International, Army, and Schoolboy days such as, Roger Byrne, Tommy Taylor, Duncan Edwards, David Pegg, and Mark Jones. When the match did finally come around two weeks later, there was no way Sheffield Wednesday could have won, the whole country was behind United, and I suppose so were the rest of my own side."*

Tickets were being sold and special trains from Sheffield to Manchester booked, when the news began to filter through that the plane carrying Manchester United back from Belgrade had crashed. Initial reports were sketchy at best, but numerous fatalities were being mentioned.

The cold reality of what had occurred became clearer the following day. Seven United players – Eddie Colman, Roger Byrne, Tommy Taylor,

Mark Jones, David Pegg, Liam Whelan and Geoff Bent, along with trainer Tom Curry, coach Bert Whalley and secretary Walter Crickmer were all killed, as were eight journalists, one crew member and two other passengers. Others lay injured in hospital, with Duncan Edwards, later to die from his injuries.

It was a disaster that affected not just Manchester United, but British football as a whole, if not the whole sporting world. The England international side felt the pain of losing the likes of Roger Byrne, David Pegg, Tommy Taylor and the colossus that was Duncan Edwards.

The events of that afternoon had telling effect on Albert and were, although unknown at the time, to change his life.

The scheduled FA Cup tie was postponed, as it would have been totally unfair and unjust for the Football Association to expect Manchester United to field a team in such circumstances. Yes, they had reserves and a clutch of promising youths, but only two of the survivors, Harry Gregg and Bill Foulkes were in any fit state, physically, to play. Rescheduling the game for Wednesday February 19th, it allowed Manchester United some breathing space.

So, instead of lining up to face Manchester United at Old Trafford in the FA Cup, Albert and his team mates were locking horns with Chelsea in a First Division fixture at Hillsborough on February 15th. It wasn't to be the best preparation for what lay ahead at Old Trafford four days' later, but it was to see Albert back amongst the goals, converting two penalties in the 3-2 defeat. Jimmy Greaves stole the headlines with a hat-trick.

The coach journey made by the Wednesday team across the Pennines from Sheffield to Manchester on the afternoon of February 19th must have been a solemn one. The usual joviality replaced by silence as they contemplated not just the ninety minutes, but what actually lay ahead in a city still mourning its loss. They would have been more than aware that they were about to enter something akin to a proverbial lion's den. They were also aware that this was a game that they could not win, no matter what. It wasn't simply the odds that were stacked against them, the whole country wanted Manchester United to win.

Albert was to recall: *"Before the game started, I managed to have a quick word with Bobby Charlton who had just returned from Munich, and moments later I led my team down the tunnel, after the United side.*

"Never could the emotion of the evening have hit anybody harder. Two of the United players had been plucked from their third team, Mark Pearson and Seamus Brennan, and they were making their debuts in the first team. Incredibly, it was those two youngsters who caused all the problems! Shay scored direct from a corner and I am

sure that the massive crowd blew the ball in! Brennan also got the second, before Pearson, who was a Sheffield lad, opened us up for Alex Dawson to make it three. To be honest, the game was a blur; United managed to play some football despite the emotion, and deservedly knocked us out."

Albert played as any captain would, trying to generate something from what was always a losing battle. He did his best to stir a Wednesday attack that was up against a defence who were a step or two quicker to the ball. Coupled with United's free flowing front line and backed by a constant wall of noise, it was a fruitless cause. Even the haunting pre-match minute's silence would have been enough to sow the seeds of doubt into the minds of the most strongly willed Wednesday players, that this was to be a football match like no other.

On paper, the United side put together by Jimmy Murphy – Munich survivors Gregg and Foulkes, the makeshift signings of Ernie Taylor and Stan Crowther, who would have been totally unfamiliar to his team mates as he was only signed late that same afternoon, reserve team players Greaves, Goodwin, Cope and Webster, along with the youngsters Dawson, Pearson and Brennan, should have been beatable, even by the lacklustre Sheffield Wednesday. Perhaps on another day, but not on this occasion.

Wednesday recovered from their haunting ninety minutes at Old Trafford, taking four points from their next three games. A 1-0 defeat away at Birmingham City failed to make it four unbeaten, but momentum was restored thanks to Albert's goal in the 1-0 win over Bolton Wanderers. It was, however, to be only momentary, as the following Saturday saw another point-less ninety minutes with a 1-0 defeat at Highbury against Arsenal.

Despite Wednesday's lowly League status and Albert's subsequent departure from the England scene, he remained a pin-up boy. Newspaper articles, covering Sheffield Wednesday in general, would more often than not, be accompanied with a photograph of him, while the Barnsley British Co-operative secured his services for four days between 2.30pm and 9.00pm at their 'Sports & Camping Exhibition' in the local Arcadian Banqueting Hall in the town's Market Street. The only day between Tuesday March 25th and Monday March 31st that he was not making an appearance was Saturday the 29th.

On that last Saturday in March, he had a more pressing appointment and one that could in hindsight have been the turning point of Albert Quixall's footballing career. It was an afternoon that saw Manchester United make the journey to Hillsborough on League business. There were no thoughts of revenge in the air, simply the need for two points in the battle against relegation. The 1-0 defeat at Highbury had knocked Wednesday back to the foot of the table and prior to the visit of Manchester United, they remained there, a point worse off than Newcastle United, two adrift of Sunderland, while three points separated them from Leicester City, Aston Villa and Portsmouth.

Against Manchester United in what was described as the hardest and most thrilling game played at Hillsborough so far that season, Albert produced a performance up there with his best. Denied the opening goal in the fourteenth minute by a linesman's raised flag, he took the game by the scruff of the neck, was at the heart of every move and caused United all sorts of problems, creating what was to be the only goal of the match for Shiner five minutes before half time.

It had been four years since his last England cap, but on such showings, another outing in the white shirt was due. What could be forgotten was that he was still only twenty-three, nearing maturity in footballing terms, but with Wednesday in the footballing doldrums and the likes of Johnny Haynes, Derek Kevan and Jimmy Greaves also in the international picture, a player from the First Division basement was far from being a priority.

Despite that 1-0 triumph over Manchester United and a final day 2-1 victory over champions Wolverhampton Wanderers, Sheffield Wednesday were doomed, returning once again to the Second Division, their fourth visit to the second tier of the English game since the Second

World War. It was to be the nail on the coffin for manager Eric Taylor, as, by the time the new season came around, former Rochdale manager Harry Catterick was in charge, with Eric Taylor stepping into an administrative role.

An ankle injury received in a practice match denied Albert his place in the Wednesday side for the 1958-59 season opener against Swansea Town and also for the half dozen fixtures that followed, with his first outing of the season not coming until Saturday September 6th against Bristol Rovers, marking his return by scoring in the 3-1 victory. It was the first of only four starts he was to make for Sheffield Wednesday that season.

With the 1958-59 season underway and Albert Quixall kicking his heels on the touchline, itching for a return to the fray, new Wednesday manager Harry Catterick was well aware that an immediate return to the First Division was of the utmost priority. By mid-September, the statistics were favourable – played eight, won six, drew one, lost one and sitting comfortably in second place, but there was a dark cloud hovering over Hillsborough.

Following the *'was he – wasn't he'* tapping saga of September 1957, all had been quite in regards to Albert Quixall's Sheffield Wednesday future, but midway through September 1958, the matter once again reared its head, with manager Harry Catterick telling Peter Lorenzo of the *Daily Herald "I suspect that at least one big club has been tapping Quixall. Something is certainly worrying him. He hasn't been playing as well as he can.*

"I've had a talk with him. I told him – so that we could know where stood – that if he wanted to leave Wednesday, he should say so. If he had said he wanted leave and gave certain reasons, I have no doubt it would have to be considered. But he told he was quite happy with us.

"It's a strange thing, Quixall has first-class wages and conditions Hillsborough. No other League club can look after him better within the bounds of regulations."

With the seeds sown, the sports pages of the following day had latched onto the possibility of Albert leaving Sheffield Wednesday. *"Are You Listening Busby And Brown – Quixall Price Tag is £30,000"* was the follow-up heading to the previous day's story in the *Daily Herald*. The article below it read: *"Sheffield Wednesday will part with the one-time wonder-boy, Albert Quixall. But they want big money – at least £30,000 – for their 25-year-old inside forward. Manchester United and Sunderland are likely to lead the bidders.*

"For many years Wednesday have thundered: 'We won't sell Quixall at any price.' Now, after the he's-been-got-at outburst from the club yesterday, comes the first suggestion that they are planning to do business.

"*Last night secretary Eric Taylor announced: 'If we did let him it would have to be the biggest-ever deal for one our players. I doubt if any club could pay the money we want for him'* "

John Bromley, whose name accompanied the article continued by saying that the player had been unsettled for the past couple of seasons, adding that he had also been inconsistent on the field, often dazzling, but sometimes only dabbling, that Wednesday's yo-yo form had been the main trouble.

Albert himself was non-committal when approached. *"I'm very happy with Sheffield Wednesday. I have not asked for a transfer and no club has approached me. I know Sheffield Wednesday are in the red. So, if they feel they could solve their problems by transferring me, I would willingly go to help them out. But I would much rather return to First Division soccer with the rest of my teammates."*

Obviously being a life-long supporter of the club, he would want to see them back in the top flight, but the revelation that Wednesday were in the red and his admission of being willing to leave was a clear green light to any interested clubs.

He had no shortage of suitors, as a queue was quick in forming. George Swindon, manager of Arsenal immediately said he was interested, but would need a check on his form. Aston Villa, looking for a forward made an early enquiry. Birmingham City chairman Harry Morris declared that the money was there, as did Bob Dennison of Middlesbrough. The early favourites, however, were Manchester United, eager to re-build following the Munich disaster, with manager Matt Busby saying: *"He is not on the transfer-list yet. When, and if he is, we would be very interested. We are interested in all good players, and Quixall is certainly a good player"*

"*I would join them if they wanted me,*" was all Albert would say, although he was also quick to add that he would only move, if such a scenario arrived, to a First Division club.

The expected transfer request came on Tuesday September 16th 1958 and although his star didn't shine quite so brightly as it had done in the past, Albert Quixall was still very much subject matter that could fill a few column inches and sell a few extra newspapers, so it was only expected that his current situation was exploited to the full when details of the request were issue, and it was not surprising that his name was all over the sports pages on the morning of September 17th. "*Busby May Buy £30,000 Quixall*" shouted the *Daily News (London)*. "*We'll Have A Go For Quixall, Says United Chairman*" – *Newcastle Evening Chronicle*. "*United May Top £35,000 For Quixall*" – *Daily Mirror* and "*City v United – For Quixall's Signature*" – *Manchester Evening News*, only a few of the examples.

In the wake of transfer request, Eric Taylor said: *"Albert has no grouse or grumble against Wednesday or anyone connected with the club, but he thinks he has a better chance of furthering his career by playing in the First Division. The request will be considered at the next meeting of the directors."*

Having nurtured Albert since he was a mere schoolboy, Sheffield Wednesday might well have felt let down by the request from their star player and biggest asset, but the request came at a time when everything was in their favour.

Wednesday had started their Second Division programme in top form with only one defeat in the opening seven games and had been playing well without Albert in the side.

Somewhat strangely, in the wake of that transfer request and the furore that followed, the name Quixall appeared in the Wednesday line-up to face Sunderland hours after the aforementioned headlines appeared on the newsstands. But neither the player himself, nor his teammates were affected in any way, as they hit Sunderland for six, with Albert scoring one of the goals.

His performance against the Roker Park side left no doubts as to commitment to Sheffield Wednesday while still on their books, and it was considered that it had in fact added another £1,000 on to his eventual transfer fee.

It was now simply a case of 'when', not 'if' he would leave, as the Wednesday directors wasted little time in agreeing that he could leave, as long as the transfer fee was a suitable one.

There was, however, only going to be one winner in the race for his signature. In the article that appeared in the *Manchester Evening News* of September 17th and written by Eric Thornton, the paper's City correspondent and David Meek, his United counterpart, with the paper having mentioned that City had joined the race for Albert's signature, they wrote: *"But when the player signs – probably tonight – it will be for Manchester United."* It continued: *"We expect a deal to be clinched tonight, immediately after the game against Sunderland – and that United will be the club to pull it off.*

"Everything is in United's favour. Cash presents no problem to them. The player has said that he would rather go to Old Trafford than anywhere else. Manchester is within easy travelling distance of Quixall's home town."

With the rubbish still being swept off the Hillsborough terraces and stands the morning after that victory over Sunderland, Matt Busby, accompanied by director Louis Edwards and secretary Les Olive were heading to Sheffield along with a cheque book, Busby having already been over the Pennines the previous night to set the ball rolling. A mere twelve hours had passed since Albert's transfer request had been granted, with the signing itself taking no more than half an hour.

It might only have taken some thirty minutes to conclude the deal, but it a mere minute of Matt Busby meeting Eric Taylor for the Wednesday man to let the United manager know what was what. *"Take a deep breath Matt, I'm going to shake you,"* said Taylor. *"We want £45,000."*

"I knew I would have to pay a big fee," Busby admitted later, *"but I didn't expect it to be that big.*

"However, I went to the phone, contacted my board in Manchester, and then rejoined the Sheffield people.

"Take a deep breath yourself Eric," I said. *"I've just spoken to my directors and I'm going pay you what you want."*

Once the deal had been concluded, Busby added: *"It is well known we have been building since the Munich disaster. I have always been a great admirer of this boy. I think he will be a great asset and the foundation of our rebuilding policy which will take us back to the top.*

"I am delighted to have Albert on my books. He will play at inside right against Spurs at Old Trafford on Saturday. After the match he will go with us to Interlaken, where we shall be staying for the match with the Boys of Berne."

"This is a big moment for me" exclaimed Albert. *"This is the club that I most wanted to join. I am looking forward to a long and happy future at Old Trafford.*

"Harry Catterick called me into his office to meet Matt Busby. I signed virtually straight away without knowing the fee and went off to play golf. Soon all hell broke loose, with hordes of reporters and photographers chasing me from hole to hole.

"*Later that evening, I was over in Manchester and appeared on the 'Tonight' television programme with Cliff Mitchelmore, that was when the record fee really hit me. It seemed for a while as if the whole world was on fire.*"

Speaking to Ben Wright of the *Daily Mirror* following his impromptu television appearance he added; "*Of course I am not worth all that money. But I am very happy to be joining Manchester United and shall do my best to live up to their high standard.*"

Taylor and Quixall

"*My wife and I are particularly happy that United have agreed to allow us to continue to live in Sheffield where we have so many ties and we are very grateful to Wednesday for allowing us to stay on in their club house until we are able to rent another.*"

Saddened to have lost the player, Eric Taylor added: "*It's a tragedy that Albert wants to leave Wednesday and Sheffield where he has learnt all his football and proved such a great player. But it was his choice. We all wish him well and will watch his progress with great interest.*"

But what of the transfer fee? As always, it depended what newspaper you read. £37,500 said the *Leicester Evening Mail*, £40,000 said the Manchester Evening News. Wolves had stepped in with a late £30,000 plus a player offer, but in the end, it was revealed that Manchester United, anxious to claim the much sought after signature, had forked out a record breaking £45,000 to get there man, £10,000 more than the previous record that took Cliff Jones to Tottenham from Swansea Town.

"*I admit I was surprised when the Quixall price was revealed. A £25,000 fee.... yes. Even £30,000.... but the ceiling price of £45,000 is almost into the realms of fantasy,*" said former Everton player and now Sheffield United manager Joe Mercer.

"Make no mistake. Quixall is a good player. I've been plugging his cause for years. The move to Manchester United will be the best thing that has ever happened to him.

"In the Old Trafford set-up, Quixall can develop into a 'great.' At the moment, he tends to be rather a one-way player, going out of the game for spells, but United boss Matt Busby knows all the wrinkles and Quixall will be brought to his peak in exalted company."

The news of the transfer wasn't simply spread across the back pages of the national press, as it commanded a share of the front pages as well. *"Golden Boy Quixall – In Fact He's Worth Twice his Weight In Gold"* appeared on the front page of the *Daily Herald* along with a photograph of the player and a breakdown of what the transfer fee meant. Weighing eleven stone, the *Herald* reckoned that if he was worth his weight in gold then it would work out at £12 10s. per ounce, which actually amounted to only £23,100, about half the transfer fee.

A further breakdown stated that if he averaged twenty goals per season, it would work out at £225 a goal. A playing life of ten seasons would be £4,500 per season. Measuring 5' 7 in height, it was £671 per inch and at 11 stone in weight it was £18 5s per ounce. His on-field appearances would work out at 25s. per minute and over forty games a season, that would be £112 10s. per match. Finally, it was down to £22,500 a leg! All trivial amounts by today's standards.

When asked why he had paid £45,000 for Albert Quixall, Matt Busby reply was: *'We play to capacity crowds at Old Trafford. In fairness to them, we must always try to give them the best in football entertainment. A player like Quixall will help keep the crowd happy – and a club's duty is to have the money on the field rather than in the bank. It's good business besides."*

The news of the transfer wasn't the only mention of Albert Quixall in the national press on September 19th, as there was also a mention of him having been fined at Wakefield that day for speeding. Although he denied doing thirty-five miles per hour, he was found guilty and later said: *"It is the first offence of any kind I have ever been charged with in three years of driving."* His punishment? A £3 fine.

Having paid that record breaking fee for Albert Quixall, Matt Busby had to now fit him into his team and it was more than likely that the man who would be losing his place was the veteran, Ernie Taylor, who had come in and did a sterling job immediately after Munich. Albert's impeding arrival did little to concern the former Newcastle United and Blackpool inside forward and indeed, had the opposite effect. Having arrived in Manchester the day prior to his debut against Tottenham Hotspur, the first person to greet him was the thirty-three-year-old Ernie

Taylor, going as far to invite him to his house. *"I have not given it a thought,"* he replied when asked about the threat to his United first team place. *"I shall make Quixall, Charlton and Viollet play for their places. But whatever happens, I am happy to play in any team Matt Busby wants. My future is with Manchester United and I am very happy here. I'd play right back for the reserves if Matt Busby asked me."*

On the day when Jackie Blanchflower, a player who could have been lining up alongside Albert, announced his enforced retirement from the game due to injuries received in the Munich disaster, all eyes were on Old Trafford and Manchester United's match against Tottenham Hotspur.

Quixall's MUFC debut

"I have had the jitters for the past two days and have not slept well," Albert told reporters on the eve of that September 20th debut. *"But I am sure everything will be all right once I start playing football. Now that I am training, I feel better already.*

"I did not ask for the high price transfer tag. It worries me now, but I do not think it will on the football field."

For the neutral, there was only one the First Division fixture of interest on September 20th and that was between Manchester United and Tottenham Hotspur at Old Trafford. In the sports papers of that Saturday night, the Sunday titles of the following day and the dailies of the Monday, there was little interest in what had been a goal fest of an afternoon: six at Upton Park, five at Highbury, Burnden Park and Goodison Park and four at all the others except for Portsmouth which only produced three and Villa Park where the paying public were treated to a meagre two. All the interest circled around one man – Albert Quixall.

The headlines that followed that first ninety minutes certainly didn't stretch to proclaiming the arrival of the new messiah or anything close, as United were held to a 2-2 draw by the White Hart Lane side, both goals coming from Welshman Colin Webster, in what was considered a far from compelling ninety minutes, which were arguably over-hyped by Albert's debut.

"Quixall and His 38 Kicks Fall Short of £45,000" was the headline above Denis Lowe's report in the *Daily News*, the journalist going on to say: *"Albert Quixall was Manchester United's best forward in this disappointing draw at Old Trafford; disappointing because Spurs should have won, and because Mr Quixall did not live up to his £45,000 valuation. But Quixall, remember, was being watched like a microscopic specimen by the 62,036 spectators. I followed him with my pencil poised, my note book ready, watching his every move.*

"These statistics, however, must be related to two facts when assessing Quixall – the many shortcomings of his team mates and the close attentions paid him by another Sheffield exile, Jim Iley, who cost Spurs £15,000.

"Starting from the 20th second of the match, when Quixall lofted a pass for Alex Dawson to chase, he was in possession of the ball 38 times – 18 in the first half, 20 in the second – hardly enough for a key inside forward.

"He contributed very little in defence, spending most of the match waiting up field, while Bobby Charlton toiled in vain in the rear as the schemer-in-chief.

"Quixall's big moment came when he neatly side-stepped Iley to place a perfect centre on Colin Webster's head for United's first goal.

"His personal tally of goal efforts included six shots or headers, one of which brought a fine save from John Hollowbread, but he missed a glorious chance of scoring the winner three minutes from time, only half-hitting his shot after shaking off two defenders.

"Passes? Quixall was accurate with them 29 times. Dawson should have turned at least three of them to better account. But Quixall sent out nine bad passes, and lost the ball in tackles seven times. Two free kicks were awarded for fouls against him, and he conceded one.

"The Old Trafford crowd saw enough to know that Quixall is a mere mortal after all, but I am sure he will settle down to become a key man in United's attack, providing strategy and striking power."

Harry Peterson of *The People* was of the opinion that Albert would do well over the course of time. *"He showed neat touches, clever distribution and had an eye for an opening. With poor support, he did all that could be expected in strange company. And there's no doubt that before long he will not only make goals,*

but score them. Once United recapture that slick, quick-moving brand of soccer, you can bet Quixall will quickly pay off that costly fee. His style of play is United's style... And he'll fit in like the final piece of a giant jig-saw."

The supporters were also satisfied with that initial viewing – *"He'll do,"* being the general opinion. While the man who paid out that record-breaking fee, United manager Matt Busby, was highly delighted with his new signing's performance. *"He's a great player and had a good game. Obviously, he will take time to settle in, but I'm convinced that he will do us a lot of good."*

As for the player himself, *"I thoroughly enjoyed my first outing. Now I'm looking forward to the game in Berne. For, by then, we should have worked out a few surprises for the opposition and ironed out any difficulties which may have been evident today."*

With the nerve-tingling debut out of the way and although that £45,000 tag would be round his neck for some considerable time, it would have been assumed that the furore surrounding the transfer would slowly fade into the background. But it wasn't to be. While the reports of his debut took up the column inches on the back pages, "Quixall" was also to appear on the front pages, but with no mention of the ninety minutes against Tottenham Hotspur a matter of hours earlier.

In modern times, there would have been a huge "EXCLUSIVE" banner heading, but although plumb-centre on its front page, the heading: "QUIXALL PROBE SHOCKS UNITED – CLUB FACES £45,000 DEAL ENQUIRY" was no bigger than any of the others on the front of the *Weekly Despatch* of Sunday September 21st, with Sports Editor, J. L. Manning, writing: *"Manchester United, who last week signed Albert*

Quixall for a record £45,000 fee, face a Football League investigation into charges of star poaching.

"The League's Management Committee suspects that the technique used to whisk Quixall from Sheffield Wednesday was against, at least, the spirit of the rules.

"But despite this, the United, I understand, are preparing for even bigger deals, one of which will be for the £65,000 Welsh international John Charles, at present with the Italian club Juventus.

"Here are the other main points of a sensationally developing story which will come as a shock to the football world –

"1. Manchester United are ready to refute the League's charge and to say that, far from luring Quixall from Sheffield, it was the Wednesday club who provoked the transfer because they needed the money.

"2. Smarting from the League's ban on their European Cup entry this season. the Manchester club plan to play either Juventus, or Real Madrid, three times European Cup winners, at Old Trafford next month as part of a plan to raise money for stars. Including Charles.

"The League fear big-money raids by Manchester United on other clubs. Their only hope of stopping players being lured to Old Trafford would be under-the-counter payments.

"This will start a Soccer rat-race. Already the champions, Wolverhampton Wanderers, are pressing for an investigation into transfers because their players are becoming restless. Arsenal are being watched too. Their manager, George Swindin, and Matt Busby, manager of the United, have angered the League by recent statements that they 'would like' certain players."

The finger pointing didn't, however, last more than a few hours, as the sports pages of Monday September 22nd were quick to reveal that the reports of an investigation into Albert Quixall's transfer were being denied, with the president of the Football League, Mr. Joe Richards, saying that he knew nothing about it. United chairman Mr. Harold Hardman said likewise. *"We do not know anything about an investigation. We have heard nothing. We've got nothing to fear and nothing to hide. The whole thing is without foundation. I think someone had a bad dream."* Sheffield Wednesday general manager Eric Taylor added: *"My club has certainly made no move, nor are we interested in doing so."*

With the dust seemingly settled, Albert decided that the time was now right to speak out about his transfer.

"How much do you think Matt Busby slipped me to join Manchester United? How big do you think the under-counter payment was?

"Nearly everyone I meet seems convinced that I made a lot of money on this transfer. They nudge each other, give me a wink, and say I should be all set up now.

"Well, let's get this straight… I did not receive an illegal penny.

"I suspect that in football many players over the years have received some form of back-hander. But as soon as negotiations for me started, Mr Busby made it quite clear to me that I need not expect any kind of bribe.

"Actually, he need not have bothered to tell me, because the word goes round among players about this kind of thing and I did not expect anything over the odds.

"Probably a lot of the football know-alls will still believe I made my fortune leaving Sheffield Wednesday for the famous United – but they are barking up the wrong tree."

Financial inducements and brown envelopes were a thing for the distant future.

Although there was some initial concern regarding the fee United paid out, if there had been even the slightest hint of wrongdoing then they could have been guaranteed to have had the Football League hammering on their door.

There had been no love lost between Manchester United and the Football League ever since the football club had gone against the governing body when accepting that initial invitation to take part in the European Cup. Having persuaded Chelsea not to take part in the 1955-56 competition, the League found United a much tougher egg to crack and Matt Busby persuaded his board to turn their back on the League and grasp the invitation firmly with both hands.

Having been shunned like an unwanted suitor, the League never forgot United's stance and when another invitation arrived through the Old Trafford letter box in the summer of 1958, inviting them to take part in the 1958-59 European Cup, the Football League once again stepped in and stamped their feet and said "NO", despite United having been given the go-ahead by the Football Association.

"I refuse to say anything at all about Manchester United," said Alan Hardacre, totally riled by public opinion. Even after an appeal was upheld by the Football Association, allowing United to take part in the competition, Hardacre and his co-members stood firm, going as far to suggest that they would ban United from playing First Division football in the 1958-59 season if they took part in the European Cup.

Suddenly, the matter was taken out of United's hands when the Football Association, for one reason or another, backtracked and informed the club that they were refused permission to enter the European competition on the basis that they were not League champions in that 1957-58 season.

So that was it. The door was slammed shut in United's face and if indeed any wrong-doing could have been found in the handling of the

Albert Quixall transfer by Manchester United, then it could have been assumed they would have been hauled across the coals quicker than you could said 'sign here.' The suggestions of any inappropriate approaches, brown envelopes or whatever, were to disappear as quickly as they had arisen.

With his debut out of the way, Albert was able to relax slightly before heading to Switzerland with his new team mates to face Berne Young Boys, but, before his departure, there was yet another contract to sign, one with the *Manchester Evening News*, which would see him write a weekly column for the local newspaper.

In regards to this regular column in the *Evening News*, Albert was to say: *"If not for the money received writing in the Manchester Evening News, I would have difficulty paying my way in comfort."* Such columns were considered to be worth around £30 a week to the individual fortunate enough to offer his thoughts on the game for the newspaper's large readership.

His first contribution was to see him reflect on his transfer, of which he wrote: *"I would not say that Sheffield Wednesday wanted to get rid of me – but they certainly made my transfer easy. What a contrast to a year ago when I first asked for a move.*

"Then, every argument imaginable was used to persuade me to stay in Sheffield. This time when I asked to go on the transfer list I was put on like a shot. I suppose Wednesday needed the money. Do not think I have any grumbles with my old club. They always treated me excellently. I also owe them a big debt because they are the only club I have been with."

He continued: *"I have always admired Manchester United, and once I had decided to ask for a move there was only one club for me. I always enjoyed playing against them. The man who used to mark me was, of course, Duncan Edwards. I knew Duncan as a pal. We did a couple of tours for England together and hit up a friendship. He was a powerhouse of a player but dead fair on and off the field.*

"I liked playing against him because if I held my own, I knew I must have had a good game.

"Then came that bizarre game against United after the crash. The atmosphere was electric. It was like playing against two teams. That game drove home for me the tremendous spirit that exists at Old Trafford. Everything has come up to expectations too. The lads are a great bunch and have made me very welcome."

The fixture against Berne could have been a first round European Cup tie had the English football authorities not intervened and showed little in the way of compassion to United's immediate post-Munich problems. It doesn't bear thinking about, what they would have done had United been awarded the European Cup as a gesture towards the end of that mind numbing 1957-58 season as had been suggested by the likes of Real Madrid. However, with United and the Swiss club having been in negotiations regarding the never-to-materialise cup ties, they decided to play each other home and away in friendlies.

Making his second appearance in a red shirt, Albert was to find it far from being a friendly, as his opposite number, the six-foot-tall Heinz Schneiter, showed little regard for the record transfer fee, nor indeed Albert Quixall, as he constantly fouled him during the home side's 2-0 victory, whilst having done so, mockingly apologised.

A £45,000 transfer, or playing for Manchester United, might have promised much, but it certainly did not guarantee selection for the national side and his name was nowhere to be seen when the selectors announced the squad to face Ireland in Belfast and a Football League side to face the Scottish League in Glasgow in October 1958. He was now well down the pecking order behind the likes of Peter Broadbent of Wolves, Johnny Haynes of Fulham, Jimmy Greaves of Chelsea and Ray Parry of Bolton. There was even a call-up for Derek Wilkinson of Sheffield Wednesday at outside right in the League side, someone who had benefitted from Albert's transfer.

Luck, however, was on Albert's side, as an injury to Ray Parry whilst playing for Bolton against Preston North End saw him recruited into the Football League side, but the 1-1 draw on the banks of the Clyde did nothing to re-establish his international credentials as his performance failed to make any impression on those who mattered. Indeed, three days after his appearance for the Football League, the South Shields *Football Gazette* carried the following: *"Albert Quixall has been a Busby Babe for only three weeks now, and during that time his performances for United have hardly warranted a £45,000 tag. Has it turned out that his signing was a Busby blunder?*

"Busby can be credited with phenomenal knowledge of soccer and star-grooming, but how long can United afford to play an out-of-form Quixall when Ernie Taylor and Mark Pearson are back to their goal snatching best?

"Perhaps it will lead to Quixall losing his place. He was overshadowed by Pearson, who had a brilliant game against Wolves on Saturday night. And remember United have not won since Quixall joined them, whereas, with Taylor at inside right, United blazed off to a great start.

"Centre forward Dennis Viollet is not getting the service which saw him grab goals so impressively at the start of the season.

"It looks then as though Quixall is finding it hard to settle in at Old Trafford, and he may not do so before it is too late."

The ramifications of the £45,000 transfer failed to disperse and the move was once again thrown into the public domain and to the feet of the Football League regarding whether or not Albert was due to be paid £300 as his share of the fee. Complications arose from the fact that while Wednesday were willing to sell him, he had also asked for a transfer, with the League regulations stating that the £300 should only be paid to players who had not asked for a move.

Although he had said that he had made no money from his transfer from Sheffield Wednesday to United, it was to be proved wrong as he was entitled to £300, but once again the Football League dragged their heels and it wasn't until late November that an enquiry decided that he was entitled to the money.

The spotlight continued to shine directly on Albert Quixall, perhaps more so as, following his transfer, Manchester United had gone from a mid-table placing, within two points of the leaders to dropping down a few places and finding themselves five points adrift of the top placed club. The 2-1 defeat at home to West Bromwich Albion making it seven games without a win. Fixtures against Wolves away and Preston North End at home in early October had failed to produce a goal.

If the South Shields *Football Gazette* article opened a few eyes, it was nothing compared to the one that appeared in the *Gloucester Citizen* on October 18th. This was prior to the 3-2 defeat at Everton, the sixth game without a victory, a seventh a week later following the 2-1 home defeat by West Bromwich Albion. Even in the late 1950's and despite being in the throes of a re-building process, Manchester United were still newsworthy as the *Gloucester Citizen proved*, but while the South Shields publication stretched to a couple of paragraphs, the *Citizen* covered the best part of a quarter of a page. Their correspondent Peter Blackman, however, was more positive in his writing: *"His Form Has Been Puzzling Since Joining United, But – Only A Matter Of Time Before Quixall Strikes Top Form"* was the heading that was to lead into the article which saw Blackman write that a cloud appeared to be forming over Albert's head and the player himself was battling gamely with his personal crisis of not having settled down at Old Trafford.

He continued: *"It would be a gigantic task to attempt to pin-point the reason why Quixall has not registered immediate glory with United.*

"Many critics are of the opinion that the transfer fee has sapped his on and off the field confidence. They are saying, and with some justification, that the money tag is weighing too heavily on his shoulders.

"Another factor – to me this is more important and nearer the mark – is that Quixall's role at Sheffield was vastly different to that expected of him at Old Trafford. At Hillsborough the restless Quixall was regarded as a specialist. He also knew, thoroughly, the role he had to play. But with United he had to disband this technique for the all-round style made famous by Matt Busby.

"Quixall is now required to open up his game and work more closely with his teammates. This change of style is the major factor behind his momentary failure to blend effectively with the United."

He concluded: *"It will be only a matter of time before Quixall – everybody's buddy in football – becomes a Busby Babe in every sense of the word; and is knocking on the England door again."*

Blackman was to be proved only partly correct.

Manchester United's dismal start to the 1958-59 season was certainly not down to the signing of Albert Quixall. Munich, a taboo word around Old Trafford, was still fresh in the memories, with the scars still to heal. A 2-1 victory over Leeds United at Elland Road brought sighs of relief, but seven days later it was a return to the norm with a 3-1 defeat against Burnley at Old Trafford. The only plus point of an otherwise dismal afternoon was in Albert opening his United scoring account.

Many were now of the opinion that the corner had finally been turned, for both player and team, but those thoughts soon vaporised as a short journey out of Manchester to Bolton ended in a 6-3 thrashing.

However strange it may seem, that defeat did see the corner turned. Busby, having contemplated long and hard team selections over the opening weeks of the season, had introduced winger Warren Bradley, a 'gift' signing from North East amateur side Bishop Auckland in the wake of the Munich disaster, into the outside-right spot for that disastrous ninety minutes against Bolton with the diminutive number seven turning in a more than creditable performance. Dennis Viollet, who had missed the previous four fixtures through injury and having previously worn that number seven shirt in a handful of fixtures, returned to the fray against Luton Town on November 22nd at centre forward and everything clicked.

Viollet wasn't a winger and neither was Albert's previous partner on the right, Colin Webster, but the introduction of Bradley proved to be a refreshing tonic for him, as was Viollet on his other side, and neither player or team looked back following that 2-1 victory over Luton.

From a pre-Luton statistical review of: played eighteen, won five, lost eight, drawn five, the floodgates opened and between that November 23rd fixture and the end of the season it was a case of played twenty-four, won nineteen, lost three and drawn two. A remarkable turnaround, which was to see United finish in second place, only five points adrift of champions Wolves. It was not only a remarkable turnaround, but a remarkable achievement considering the events surrounding the club over the past fourteen months.

As 1958 drew to a close, 'beginning to live up to his £45,000 transfer fee,' were the words being thrown across the newspaper columns like confetti; however, just like in his Hillsborough days, the only thing missing were the goals, his total for the season being a mere four from thirty-three outings. Despite that lack of goals, many were of the opinion that Albert was back in contention for an England call-up, but it was never to happen.

Others were no so complimentary, especially following the shock 3-0 defeat at Norwich in the FA Cup. *"One critic said after the Norwich match that Bobby Charlton and I walked through the game with the disdain of concert pianists asked to play honky-tonk. I can't agree with that. We wanted to win that game more than any other this season and we tried our hardest.*

"My only complaint is the ice-bound pitch which, to put it bluntly, reduced us to Third Division level.

"Perhaps I am a big-head, but if we could not beat Norwich City on a normal pitch, I'll eat my canary for my next Sunday lunch." Thankfully Albert was long gone by February 1967, or his Sunday lunch could have been an interesting one following Norwich City's 2-1 fourth round victory in the competition at Old Trafford.

His weekly contribution to the *Manchester Evening News* supplemented his wages from Manchester United, but was also to drop him in deep water following his comments on Portsmouth's performance in their 3-1 Easter Monday defeat: *"They surprised us with the terrific fight they showed (United had beaten them 6-1 at Old Trafford three days previously). But I wonder how much of their trouble stems from backstage unhappiness which exists at Fratton Park?"*

These words were not well received when brought to the attention of Portsmouth manager, Freddie Cox, and it took an apology from Matt Busby and Albert to douse the flames. Busby was to add: *"Naturally, I cannot control these things. Albert may have heard something from somebody. I don't know."*

CHAPTER SIX
ABOARD THE UNITED ROLLERCOASTER

Away from football, the summer months brought out Albert's talent as a cricketer, a sport he had always enjoyed. As a Sheffield Wednesday player, he had often played in charity matches, with one such outing against Gainsborough Britannia, seeing him twenty-five not out in a thirty-three runs victory, whilst also being credited with a catch. Prior to the start of pre-season training for the 1959-60 season, he was a member of a Manchester United side, which also included Bobby Charlton, Wilf McGuinness and Freddie Goodwin, an individual who had actually represented Lancashire, who met a South West Manchester side at Ellesmere Road in Chorlton-Cum-Hardy. The previous week had also seen him line-up for a *Manchester Evening News* side against Cheadle Hulme. But those cricket whites were soon stored away and it was down to business once again and a return to the back page headlines that seemed to have haunted him since his arrival at Old Trafford.

"*Busby Men Sent Off In Munich*" screamed those headlines, with the report below telling the readers that with United 2-0 up against Bayern Munich, Joe Carolan, having been crudely obstructed by Zsamboki the Bayern inside right, had threw his hand at the back of the players head, bringing an instant dismissal.

Having been awarded the free-kick, Albert ran across to take it, only to have the ball knocked out of his hands by the offending Zsamboki. Pushing the volatile Hungarian out of the way, an action ignored by the referee, Albert took the kick, but play was almost immediately stopped as a raised linesman's flag caught the referee's attention.

The linesman then made a kicking gesture several times in order to get his point across to the referee, who immediately proceeded to send Albert to the dressing room. A somewhat over dramatic cameraman added his own impersonation to what he had apparently seen, inflaming the situation further.

Albert's sending off overshadowed what would arguably be one of the best goals of his career, firing home from fifty-yards, four seconds into the second-half. *"I saw the goalkeeper standing on the edge of the penalty area. So, when I received the kick-off pass from Dennis Viollet, I took one stride and let fly over his head."*

Steve Richards of the *Daily Herald* was later to describe it as *"The Moment I'll Never Forget"* writing: *"Only the expected had come to pass on a sunny afternoon in Munich in 1959 when 22 footballers of Bayern F.C. and Manchester United had gone through the motions of the first half of a pre-season friendly game.*

"Albert Quixall shuffled his slender frame towards the centre circle suggesting a gross indifference to it all.

"As the referee raised his whistle to start the second half the line-up was no different from normal except that the Bayern goalkeeper had settled on the edge of the penalty area instead of under the cross-bar.

"Who cared?

"As the referee blew the whistle, United centre forward Dennis Viollet side-footed the ball 2ft. in front of Quixall, the inside right.

"With no more exertion than a cobbler raising a hammer, Quixall lifted his right foot and potted the ball – straight and true – over the goalkeeper's head and into the net first bounce.

"The applause was delayed and, when it came, reluctant and suspicious.

"Nobody could believe it had happened. Quixall's high spring of delight was released only it seemed on assurance from teammates that he had achieved the 'impossible' and scored from the half-way line without moving more than a yard.

"I dare suggest that no goal to equal it has been scored in football history.

"The ball flew over 30 yards in seconds which were not counted because of the surprise. Was it a fluke? No doubt its greatness was a natural temptation.

"Yet the shot had not been an intended long pass diverted by wind. There was no wind. It had not been a hopeful downfield punt deflected by an opponent's boot or head. No boot or head could get near it.

"In German and English, they planned to question Quixall after the match – had he intended the goal?

"It deserved gold-plated headlines. But it hardly got into print and perished because Quixall himself was ordered off by the referee in the same match.

"A sensational goal buried beneath an avalanche of comment on just another sending off. Tempers matched the burning sun. The dressing rooms were scalded by blistering words.

"Only after the inquisitors had turned their backs could I slip the other question: "Did you mean it, Albert? You know, the goal?

"Unemotionally, he replied: 'Yes. We discussed it at the interval. The goalkeeper had been on the edge of the penalty area too much. It was worth trying."

As regards the sending off: *"I thought the decision on Quixall was outrageous and I doubt if Carolan did enough for a game of this nature to have earned being sent off,"* exclaimed an annoyed Matt Busby. A ticking off would have been seen as sufficient punishment on home soil, although the German press thought otherwise. *"Quixall performed a rash act on Zsamboki behind the referee's back which would have warranted him being sent off any ground in the world"* – *Abendzeitung*.

Busby expected the two players to receive nothing more than a censure from the Football Association, but was stunned when it was announced that the Germans had reported the erring pair to the FA *"We are proceeding in the usual manner, as if they had been sent off in England"*, the authorities announced. Thankfully, as far as Albert and Manchester United were concerned, nothing more came of the matter other than a "don't do it again" slap on the wrist.

Having miraculously finished runners-up to Wolves at the end of the 1958-59 season, Manchester United were hoping to get off to a favourable start as the 1959-60 season got underway, but two defeats in the opening three games, increasing to five in the opening ten, was not what was wanted nor expected.

Goals in the 6-3 thumping of Chelsea and in the 1-1 draw with Birmingham City saw Albert get off the mark quickly and, when missing from the United line-up against Tottenham Hotspur through injury, a game that the Londoners won 5-1, David Meek of the *Manchester Evening News* was prompted to say that: *"If anyone ever thought Albert Quixall was expensive at £45,000, this match emphasises that he was really a basement bargain. His scheming was sadly missed."*

By the end of October, Albert had claimed a further three goals, pushing him back into contention for an England re-call, something that was echoed by team mate Dennis Viollet. *"I watched England go down to Sweden on TV. What a pity the man sitting next to me was Albert Quixall."*

"England's talented but young and inexperienced forward line screamed out for a player of his type… and there he was, loafing in front of the goggle box instead of helping our sadly sagging international prestige."

The "should he be in the England side" debate had lingered on for a long time and it was now the general opinion that the recall would never materialise and that he had been thrown onto the international battlefield too young and paid the price for it, having been on the casualty list for too long.

Manchester United's 1959-60 season stuttered along with little or no continuity, lurching from victory to defeat and back again with a couple of draws thrown in for good measure. Albert continued to find the net from time to time, but an injury in a friendly against Manchester City on March 12th was to see him miss the following seven fixtures due to torn fibres on a damaged ligament, which proved slow to mend.

Although missed, his absence from the United line-up had no effect on the club's overall league placing at the end of the season, as any hopes of challenging for the title had long been diminished.

The close season of 1960 saw United take off for a tour of Canada and the United States, a whirlwind twenty-nine days, taking in ten fixtures in Toronto, New York, St Louis, Vancouver, Los Angeles, San Francisco, Massachusetts and Philadelphia.

Albert's thoughts must have echoed back to the pre-season tour of the previous August and the sending off in Germany, hoping that there would be no repetition. He did, however, find himself with a small problem of which he was completely innocent and could do nothing about.

With a free day, some of the United players decided to visit Coney Island, the American equivalent to the bustling Blackpool with its Pleasure Beach. Seeking some refreshments, they made their way into a bar and asked for a beer and a sandwich. They were duly served, except for Albert, as the barman refused to give him a beer, only the sandwich, as he did not believe he was over eighteen. Eventually, another barman took pity on him and his beer was forthcoming, much to the relief of Dennis Viollet, as Albert had already told him that he was going to drink half of his!

It had been almost two years since Albert Quixall moved from Sheffield Wednesday to Manchester United and still that £45,000 transfer fee hung round his neck as if padlocked to a chain, with the key to open and remove it having been lost. With every passing mention of the player, the fee was there alongside and despite the something of a rollercoaster ride in his Manchester United career to date, there was never any hint of unhappiness. However, prior to the start of the 1960-61 season, the suggestion that Albert Quixall could be finding employment elsewhere reared its head, with the *Sheffield Star* Saturday sports edition throwing out the headline *"Will Joe Mercer Get Far With A Bid For Quixall?"*

The accompanying article went on to mention that Mercer, manager of Aston Villa, had never hidden his admiration for Albert, but any move for him depended on two things – Matt Busby being willing to let his player leave and Albert himself actually wanting to leave.

Busby, it said, would not be satisfied until he had taken Manchester United back to the top of the tree, but the author of the article, Fred Walters, believed that if there was any approach for Albert, then it would be met with his nice, pleasant smile without even words to express his inner feelings.

As for Joe Mercer, he was considered as being angry and annoyed, declaring: *"There is not a scrap of truth in it"*, while Albert, when asked to comment, replied: *"They will have to kick me out before I leave Old Trafford."*

The rumours, however, would not go away and were still hovering on the eve of the new season.

As that new season approached, Matt Busby was still seeking that winning formula, looking for that vital ingredient to remove the inconsistency that surrounded the results, as he continued to rebuild.

In the pre-season practice match at Old Trafford, which saw the expected first team take on the reserves, Busby decided to try Albert at centre forward, a position, not actually alien to him, but arguably not his preferred one. It was a kick-about that Albert was uncertain to play in, never mind play centre forward, as he had only recently received the results of an x-ray check-up on his foot injury that had been aggravated last season and had continued to cause him problems. He was, however, given the all-clear, as there were no serious complications, allowing him to resume full training.

As the makeshift centre forward in the trial, he turned in a decent performance, scoring once.

By the end of August, however, it was not Albert Quixall, centre forward, but Albert Quixall, outside right. In the opening fixture of the new season, Blackburn Rovers had defeated United 3-1 at Old Trafford, with Albert playing in his usual inside right role, while four days later, at Goodison Park, Busby's team were trounced 4-0, with the pre-match plan of Albert lining up at inside right, but almost immediately switching to the wing, allowing Johnny Giles to move inside.

Although the result failed to impress anyone but the Evertonians, Albert, who was considered man of the match, commented that he liked playing wide and was sure that things would soon improve. And they did, almost immediately, as in the return fixture at Old Trafford on August 31st, the score line was reversed.

Football back in the sixties was light years away from the game of today. The players of the period, no matter who they played for, were appreciated by supporters and there appeared to be no bias showed against those same players in the numerous regional newspapers. The *Liverpool Echo* of Saturday October 1st 1960, proving that latter point of view as it featured as No.7 in their 'Soccer Star-tistic' column: Albert Quixall. Can you imagine that same newspaper today running such a series, never mind singing the praises of a Manchester United player? "*Among the most unassuming and good-natured players in the game,*" proclaimed the *Echo*, with the feature going on to add that Albert had always disliked the tag "*the most expensive footballer in Great Britain,*" a title now bestowed on Denis Law following his transfer from Huddersfield Town to Manchester City. But looking at the statistical details that accompanied the feature, many would point to Albert's lack of goals as being something of a downside, with only 80 in 309 League games. Thankfully, as the 1960-61 season progressed that goals-scored total would increase.

That lack of goals, however, was certainly not regarded as a problem by Matt Busby and, with the Aston Villa rumour having prodded something of a hornet's nest, it did not deter other clubs from apparently sniffing around the Trafford Park area of Manchester.

October had barely made an entrance when hints of a change of clubs was again being mooted. Matt Busby was constantly on the look-out to strengthen his Manchester United side, as he considered it far from being complete, and incomparable to the side that had been decimated in Munich. One individual that he had had on his radar over the past couple of years was David Herd, son of his former Manchester City teammate Alec. Only two victories in the opening ten games of the 1960-61 season had seen him renew his interest, approaching Arsenal's manager with a straight cash deal or that of a player-exchange.

No financial offer had been made, no notice of which player or players might be made available, but the Arsenal manager was yet another admirer of Albert Quixall and had been in the running to sign him from Sheffield Wednesday, only to be trumped by Busby.

Arsenal, having been keen to sign George Eastham from Newcastle United had offered Herd as part-exchange, but Herd declined the move. The familiar Mancunian landscape may have been much more favourable.

Any thoughts of the transfer roundabout spinning favourably within the corridors of both Highbury and Old Trafford ground to an almost immediate halt when Albert put pen to paper for the *Manchester Evening News*.

"*I see Arsenal are reported to be interested in me,*" he penned. "*Well I'd like to say… I'm not interested in Arsenal. I'm with the finest club in the world now, so I'd be stupid to want to go elsewhere.*"

He continued: "*When I was young it was the ambition of many boys of my age to play for Arsenal. But not me. When I was a boy, my sights were firmly fixed on the club I eventually went to – Sheffield Wednesday. Later, I must admit Manchester United looked really attractive to me and when Arsenal and United were after me nearly three years ago the only club that attracted me was – Manchester United.*

"*And that still goes. The Gunners are great. But thank you very much, I'm more than happy where I am – with an even greater club.*"

Arsenal manager George Swindin was later to say that he didn't want Albert and were not in the least bit interested signing him.

The glamour of Manchester United was certainly enriched by the club's on-going friendship with Real Madrid; with friendlies between the two clubs arguably another plus point in Albert's on-going love affair.

With the Spaniards in town to face United at Old Trafford in mid-October 1961, an interview by Bob Ferrier of the *Daily Herald* with Ferenc Puskas must have given Albert a huge boost. He was to say: "*Quixall I would say is a very talented player. but he plays very far back. Probably he does this to build up attacks, but I think he plays too far back. Such a player has to be able to pass the ball very accurately over 30 or 40 metres.*

"*Quixall gives the impression that he tries to build attacks on dribbling runs out of these deep positions, but this will never succeed in modern football. There are not* many di Stefano's in the game, and the modern game is to beat the defence with a pass and not with the dribbling.

"*Dribbling is used only when the player is in trouble and has to create more free space for himself before making a pass.*"

Unfortunately, Albert, although making one of United's two goals, failed to turn in a match winning performance as United lost 3-2 to the Spaniards.

The outside right experiment was brought to a halt due to an ankle injury, but following his return to the side, with appearances at both inside left and inside right, he was once again drafted wide right, with his nine appearances in this position producing United's best form of the season to date with a run of six straight victories with twenty goals scored.

A 6-0 defeat against Leicester City at Filbert Street towards the end of January was to interrupt that winning sequence, but worse was to come, with a result that would haunt Albert.

Having defeated Middlesbrough 3-0 in the third round of the FA Cup, Manchester United were drawn against Sheffield Wednesday at Hillsborough, but a knee injury, received in training on the eve of the match, prevented Albert from making a return to his old stomping ground. Whether he would have made any difference to the 1-1 score line is open for debate.

Watching from the sidelines, was his allegiance split in two? If it was, then the outcome would have been satisfactory as the teams shared a 1-1 draw, taking the tie to an Old Trafford replay.

Albert was passed fit for the encounter under the Old Trafford floodlights four days later, but at the end of the ninety minutes he would have been forgiven if he had hoped that he had been sat in the stand, or better still in his living room at home, not in a red shirt with the white number seven of the back, as United were hit for seven, humbled 7-2 by a vibrant Sheffield Wednesday side.

"*I suppose one crushing defeat at Old Trafford is not the end of the world, but it's not far off!*" he was to say at the end of the ninety minutes. He was also full of praise for his former club, in particular their performance as a team. "*On the night, they were so much better than us. I'm naturally disappointed at losing, as all the lads were, especially before such a great crowd, and all we can do now is wish a great team all the best in the later rounds.*"

There was no long-lasting effect from that disastrous FA Cup defeat, although League form continued to be patchy, while Albert celebrated his return from outside right to his favoured inside position with a goal against Bolton Wanderers in a 3-1 victory, scoring again the following week in a 3-2 defeat at Nottingham Forest.

A further five goals were to follow before the curtain came down on yet another season, including a hat-trick against Burnley at Old Trafford on April 12th, a performance that was lauded by Italian agent Gigi Peronance, who was in town to finalise the details of United's end of season tour in Italy. *"It's been worth coming all the way from Italy to see Quixall's goals,"* he was to comment.

But what was it with Albert Quixall and friendlies on foreign shores? Playing for United against Tevere Roma, he once again found himself at odds with the match official. On this occasion, however, he remained on the pitch for the complete ninety minutes, with the booking coming within the opening ten minutes of the game.

The misdemeanour was an innocuous offence, his name taken by the match official for shouting to a teammate for the ball, United being pulled up four times in those opening ten minutes for such an offence. *"Everybody calls for the ball at home. But according to this referee it seems you cannot shout – you have to clap."*

Cricket once again kept Albert occupied during the close season, playing in numerous fixtures, while an ankle injury kept him out of the reach of foreign referees as his United team mates, including the newly signed David Herd, finally arriving at Old Trafford from Arsenal, set off for the club's pre-season tour with games in Munich and Vienna. He was, however, fit enough to start the season, although he was to find himself back on the right wing when United began their First Division campaign with a 1-1 draw at Upton Park against West Ham United.

As with the previous season, Manchester United failed to maintain any form of consistency, lurching from draw to victory to defeat within the opening handful of fixtures. A 6-1 victory over Blackburn Rovers on August 26th, the third game of the new season, was followed by a 2-0 defeat at Stamford Bridge, Chelsea gaining revenge for the 3-2 defeat inflicted upon them at Old Trafford the previous week.

It was an unimpressive performance in south London, leaving manager Matt Busby far from happy and, for the next fixture, an away trip to Blackpool, Albert was to find his name missing when the team list was pinned on the dressing room notice board. Dropped, for the first time in his United career. To make matters worse, his unscheduled appearance for United's Central League side, saw him pick up an injury and remain out of Busby's plans for another week.

On his demotion, he was to say: *"I am a little surprised and disappointed, but we lost at Chelsea. I suppose someone had to go and it's me. But I'll be back, in the meantime, I wish Warren Bradley* (his replacement) *all the best."*

His absence was the subject of much conversation, with Wally Dean of the *Runcorn Guardian* considering him to have been: *"United's best forward when I have seen them this season, and his skill and speed off the mark with the ball at his feet will be recognised by United before long."*

Ninety minutes was all that Albert Quixall missed, but in his daily look at all things Manchester United, David Meek, writing prior to the first derby fixture of the season against neighbours City, was of the opinion: *Probably the most disappointing forward was Albert Quixall* (in the 1-1 draw against Aston Villa) *who has already been dropped once this month.*

"In Quixall's favour is the fact that in the white-hot atmosphere of a 'derby' match, his experience and cool head could be invaluable.

"He also plays much better in the familiar surroundings of Old Trafford."

Albert played against Manchester City, United winning 3-2, but, two games later, following a 2-0 defeat at home to Wolves and a 1-1 away draw at West Bromwich Albion, another problem arose. Having come through the ninety minutes against West Bromwich apparently unscathed, he woke in the early hours of the morning two days later to find his ankle had swollen, which lead to him being sidelined for a couple of weeks.

He returned against Bolton Wanderers at Old Trafford on October 28th, a 3-0 defeat, unaware of the black clouds hovering down by the Manchester Ship Canal, as he was to play only four first team games between those ninety minutes against Bolton and the visit of West Bromwich Albion to Old Trafford on February 24th.

Matt Busby's problem at Old Trafford could be seen as a defensive one due to the defeats and the number of goals leaked, especially if you look at the three fixtures as November blended into December, when they conceded thirteen. But, scoring goals, as well as preventing them, was just as much a concern, as the same three fixtures had seen only three goals scored. A month earlier, it had been three scored in six games.

"Manchester Disunited" was one of the headlines that found its way onto the back pages.

Returning to first team action having missed three games, and playing at inside left, Albert could not have picked a worse ninety minutes in which to make his comeback than a 4-1 defeat against Burnley at Old Trafford on November 25th. *"We saw in Quixall a jaded former golden boy of no carat value on this showing,"* commented a correspondent in the *Nelson Reader*, going on to call United: *"a scrappy collection of individuals – and some of them not very good individuals at that."*

The Manchester United side that travelled along the East Lancs Road the following Saturday to face Everton at Goodison Park, was to show three changes, with the name Quixall one of those missing. Perhaps not so much 'missing,' but dropped!

Reserve team football was not something that Albert Quixall had contemplated, but in his absence from Manchester United's first team it has to said that results did improve.

With Christmas approaching, the Manchester United minus Albert Quixall situation did not go un-noticed, particularly in the North East with both Newcastle United and Middlesbrough showing more than a passing interest. Both clubs were keen to discuss the matter with Matt Busby, but the United manager was in Dublin on scouting business and his return flight to Manchester was delayed, therefore hitting any quick transfer, involving either club, on the head.

When Busby did return to Manchester and telephone calls to Trafford Park 1661 made, the United manager made it quite clear that his club: *"were not in a position to part with any player at the moment."* He was to add: *"The matter did not go beyond inquiry stage. I also pointed out although both players were figuring in the reserve team our long list of injuries this season and our position in the league would not allow me to think of releasing them* (Quixall or Dennis Viollet) *or indeed any other player who might appear surplus to our needs."*

Boxing Day saw Nottingham Forest hammered 6-3, one part of the problem had been solved. A minor blip followed in a 1-0 defeat at home to Blackpool, but it would be another eight League games before defeat was again tasted, with only six goals leaked in seven fixtures and sixteen scored. Progress was also made in the FA Cup.

Despite being in the doldrums of United's Central League side, Albert Quixall still had his admirers, with one former Sheffield Wednesday and England left-back, Ernest Blenkinsop, wishing that his former club could buy him back, even if he were to cost £90,000.

"Quixall was one of the greatest forwards England ever had and could still be better than the men who hold the present England inside spots.

"With Alan Finney at Wednesday, he formed one the smartest right-wing combinations I've ever seen. Quixall is a good carrier and fetcher of the ball and he has proved he can shoot. But above all, his change of pace which can split a defence wide open

"On all-round ability I've never seen a player of Quixall's stature. I know this view has been shared by Billy Wright and Nat Lofthouse.

"When my old teammate at Liverpool, Matt Busby, signed Quixall I thought what a good deal he had done.

"Quixall could have been out of touch because there have been too many top-class forwards at Old Trafford and after all you can have too much of a good thing in anything.

"Quixall has not enough forceful players around him to use the openings he creates. When he was at Hillsborough, he was in what could be described as largely a crude side. Even so I saw him play an outstanding game for United when they lost at Sheffield Wednesday to a penalty goal in the Cup a few years back and I have also seen him shine in reserve games, so obviously still has the class there.

"Forget about these critics who said he had too much too soon. Quixall never was a big-head and he can still win back his England team place"

Albert returned to United first team duty on January 15th at home to Aston Villa, but he was not to see an extended run in the side, as he picked up an ankle injury, which kept him sidelined until February 21st, when he returned to the side to face Sheffield Wednesday in an FA Cup fifth round replay.

A goal against Aston Villa three days later marked his return to League football, albeit at outside right, in what was the first of a run of eight games. Strangely, reverting back to his favoured inside right spot, he scored against Leicester City in a 3-1 win, which was followed three days later by a hat-trick against Ipswich Town, on this occasion as centre forward.

Just when things looked so much brighter, thoughts of leaving diminished, if they were ever there in the first place, his ankle injury once again flared up and he was not to feature again that season.

That 1961-62 season had been soul-destroying for Albert Quixall and it is difficult to define what was the biggest source of disappointment, having to endure playing reserve team football in front of meagre crowds, compared to the packed stadiums he was accustomed to, or the seemingly on-going injury problems.

Determined to be up and running, excusing the pun, for when the new season got underway, he went out and purchased a bicycle, stating: *"It's the car. I ride about in it and it is doing me no good. Next season I shall bike the seven miles to and from the Old Trafford ground every day. I am going soft."*

The difference in football between those long-forgotten sixties days and the present are emphasised clearly in the case of Albert's injury. It had been some three months since he had hurt his ankle against Ipswich Town in that 5-0 April 2nd victory and it was not until towards the end of June that he had been seen by a specialist and had it x-rayed. "A bad sprain" was the specialist's opinion, with "no serious damage" and that he should be fit in time to resume pre-season training.

A month down the line and Albert reported that he had "*never trained as hard for a new season as this one*", as he was determined to, not simply regain his fitness, but secure a place in the Manchester United starting eleven. The latter, however, was going to be far from straight forward, as Matt Busby had once again plundered the United bank account, lessening it by the sum of £115,000, to secure the signature of Denis Law from Italian side Torino.

It Albert needed a shred of good luck, then it came through the misfortune of a teammate, with Bobby Charlton being forced onto the sidelines for an estimated three months with a hernia problem.

Flanked by youngsters Johnny Giles and Ian Moir, Manchester United could boast of a forward line worth in the region of £195,000, but such an expenditure was not guaranteed to reap dividends and United's 1962-63 First Division campaign opened with only two victories in their first seven games, these were accompanied by a draw and four defeats and, despite Busby's outlay, three of those defeats failed to produce a solitary goal.

The season began with West Bromwich Albion visiting Old Trafford, returning to the Midlands happy with a point from the 2-2 draw. The same, however, couldn't said for Matt Busby, as he immediately cracked the whip, and Albert was to find himself dropped and banished back to the United reserve side. Busby continued to show his ruthless streak following the second ninety minutes of the season by dropping captain Maurice Setters, Nobby Stiles, and Mark Pearson (who had replaced Albert), following the 3-1 defeat at Goodison Park against Everton. *"We have played more than two League games,"* the United manager was to say. *"We have also played practice games and these players have not performed as well as they can."*

Albert returned to the Manchester United side for the short journey to Bolton Wanderers on September 5th, but the ninety minutes, which were to result in a 3-0 defeat, did little to endear him to Matt Busby who once again wielded the axe, dropping him for the following fixture against Leyton Orient at Brisbane Road. Another goal-less affair for United; although on this occasion they were to concede only one.

Demoted for the second time in a matter of weeks, it was the straw that finally broke the camel's back with Albert deciding that enough was enough and asked for a transfer.

"I think it would be the best thing for me and the club if I was transferred," he was to comment, adding: *"I dislike playing reserve team football and the way things have gone this season I have been very disappointed. But I am not at war with the world or anything like that because I have been dropped a couple of times. It is not true I have demanded a move, but I am concerned about my future, which seems pretty bleak at the moment."*

He was told by Busby not to bother putting his request in writing, as the pair would sit down and discuss the matter over the next couple of days and it was later agreed that should the player wish to move on, then United would not stand in his way.

Whatever Matt Busby decided to do with regards to his Manchester United team selection was entirely up to him, but it didn't necessarily mean that everyone agreed with him. One letter to the *Manchester Evening News* read: *"I am absolutely disgusted at Matt Busby's recent treatment of Albert Quixall. Mr Busby's reputation for being one of the fairest managers in football is fast becoming a thing of the past.*

"What must Quixall do to keep his place in the team – win every match single-handed? It takes eleven men to make a team, therefore surely it must take more than one man to break it. I could mention several players at Old Trafford who deserve to be dropped far more than Quixall, but their 'blue eyes' keep them in favour.

"It seems Quixall must either change the colour of his eyes or find another club. I would be extremely sorry to see Quixall go, but for his own sake, it seems to be the only solution, for no matter what he does, it isn't right." It was signed 'One Who likes Fair Play' Manchester 10.

Another supporter considered that it was worth the price of a postage stamp to put his feelings into words writing under the heading "QUIXALL THE SCAPEGOAT" – *"As a United supporter of over 30 years I am disgusted with the treatment of Albert Quixall. This season, Quixall has been no better and no worse than the rest of the forwards, but what chance can any inside forward have of playing his proper game unless he receives constructive support?*

"For most of Quixall's time with United have been bedevilled with wing-halves whose ideas of constructive football would cause raised eyebrows at the Eton Wall Game. Additionally, we have lacked a top-class right-winger (I except Giles who is not a natural winger).

"However, many inside rights are made scapegoats, nothing will improve until these basic faults are remedied. The Albert Quixall who pulverised Ipswich last season is still one the best inside forwards in the League, but it looks as if he is well advised to seek a club where he will be given a chance to prove it.

"As for me, it is TV on Saturday afternoons!" Signed E. Leetch.

Whether or not a transfer was forthcoming, as before, numerous clubs began to keep a watchful eye on the developing situation, with numerous newspapers of September 12th carrying the story that Albert was considering a move to Stoke City, with terms having been agreed between the clubs. Stoke manager, Tony Waddington, going as far as to say that it had been hoped to sign him in time to have played against Charlton that night, but Albert wanted more time to consider the move.

The 'will he, won't he' saga rumbled on for a few days, but finally came to a head on Friday September 21st when Stoke City withdrew their offer of £20,000/£25,000, opening up the opportunity for Southampton to try and persuade him to venture even further south. Albert failed to comment on the breakdown of the Stoke move, but Matt Busby was to say: *"The position remains the same so far as we are concerned. If Quixall still wants to go then we shall not stand in his way."*

Albert made something of a surprise return to the Manchester United first team line-up against Benfica at Old Trafford on Tuesday September 25th, scoring from the penalty spot in a 2-2 draw. His overall performance wasn't quite the Quixall of old, but it was a first-class display, working brilliantly alongside Denis Law, making him the major conversation point as the crowds spilled out of the Old Trafford gates and headed for home. David Meek, in the *Manchester Evening News* the following day, added fuel to the fire by asking the question that was on countless lips – *"Can manager Matt Busby still afford to let him go?"*

In the way of answer Busby said: *"It is up to the player. We would be happy to keep him, and have been all along.*

"He has been out of form, but his ability has never been in doubt. He showed that against Benfica."

As for the player himself: *"I'm still on the transfer list and a move to Stoke is still possible."*

While a move to Stoke City was considered as being "still possible," Queens Park Rangers stepped into the market place, but brought a simple *"we cannot possibly afford to part with him"* response from Manchester United and according to the *Manchester Evening News* of Monday October 15th 1962, Albert had made a renewed transfer request, but had seen it turned down by the club, leaving him *"bewildered and upset"*.

Confusion reigned.

The previous week had apparently seen Albert asking for his name to be removed from the transfer list, to which the club agreed, only for him to make a u-turn when a fit Bobby Charlton returned to first team duties against Blackburn Rovers, displacing Albert to the reserve side.

Having kicked his heels over the course of the weekend, Albert made a bee-line for Matt Busby's office on the Monday morning, demanding a transfer, only to have his request refused by Busby.

"*I cannot understand it. I thought I would have been playing in the first-team this weekend. After all, I have had only three League games this season.*

"*It does not seem as if I figure in the club's first team plans, so I think a fresh start would be best for me. I am determined to get away.*"

Wednesday October 17th saw Albert return to Manchester United first team duty at Old Trafford, but it is a fixture and a result that does not appear amongst the statistics for that 1962-63 season, the terraces and stands silent despite five goals. The fixture, against an England XI, a practice match for the national side, saw Bobby Charlton move to outside-left, allowing Albert to step into the inside right spot for the 4-1 defeat.

It was a result that mattered little, although it was to prove an important outing for Albert, as he did enough to justify his place in the side that faced Tottenham at White Hart Lane on October 24th.

"*I'm delighted to be back in the side,*" commented Albert. "*But my transfer request is still in.*"

The return to action was far from a welcome one, as the London side recorded a 6-2 victory, Albert scoring one of the two United goals from the penalty spot, extending United's run without a victory to six games, leaving them struggling in the unfamiliar second bottom place in the First Division.

Earlier in the season, such a defeat would have seen Matt Busby make wholesale changes to his starting line-up for the fixture that followed, but surprisingly, on this occasion, he didn't, perhaps well aware that due to the precarious position in the League that the club found itself in, such a decision would do more harm than good.

It was a decision that was to prove correct, as three days later, West Ham United were beaten 3-1 at Old Trafford, a result that saw Albert leave the ground with a smile on his face for the first time that season, having scored twice.

A 5-3 victory over Ipswich Town, brought a sense of normality back to Old Trafford, as did a 3-3 draw against Liverpool with Albert back in the headlines for all the right reasons, including a goal, a request for his services from Fulham having been quickly turned down by Matt Busby.

"Quixall Rips Up Liverpool Defence" was only one of the headlines, Albert's overall contribution to the ninety minutes being much more than his penalty goal. *"Quixall was brilliant throughout,"* proclaimed the *Liverpool Echo*, adding: "*his through pass which gave Herd the opening goal after thirty minutes, was the finest individual piece of work in the whole game.*"

Albert Quixall would have done anything for a quiet life. The £45,000 transfer tag would never be removed from around his neck, that was one thing that he personally could do nothing about. The on-off transfer speculation continued to follow him around like a bad smell, then in mid-December 1962, he found himself caught up in even more controversy, but this time, he was only involved on the outside, looking in.

On December 15th, Manchester United played West Bromwich Albion at the Hawthorns, a 3-0 defeat, bringing an end to an unbeaten seven game run, a notable achievement in what had been a dismal season to date. The reports of the game in the national press reflected on the game and nothing else. That was until Wednesday 19th, when all hell was let loose.

"*United Send Hot Protest Over Pullin*" and "*Manchester United To Report Pullin*" were only two of the headlines that could be found on the nation's sports pages.

It was alleged that during that 3-0 defeat at the Hawthorns, the referee, Gilbert Pullin had made unflattering remarks to Denis Law during the course of the ninety minutes, allegations that were backed by Albert.

Having listened to Law's complaint and Albert's comments, the Manchester United directorate issued the following statement: *"The directors discussed the complaint made by the players regarding remarks made by the referee during the game with West Bromwich, and decided that a strong protest be made to the Football Association and Football League."*

Matt Busby emphasised that this "strong protest" would be more than just a comment added to the official form on which clubs award marks to referees. It would be a separate letter, detailing the allegations made by Denis Law and backed up by Albert. The accompanying letter was to accuse Pullin of "heckling" Law, threatening him with disciplinary action, and making derogatory remarks about him.

To add fuel to the fire, Pullin had "previous," as recently as October, having been accused of threatening an Oxford United player during a Fourth Division fixture. On that occasion, he was cleared, this time around, he was to say that he was not worried. *"Referees and players have a lot of things to say in the course of every match,"* he added. *"But I said nothing to Law and Quixall that could possibly give offence. These complaints are silly, but I shall wait until I am asked officially before saying any more."*

Denis Law admitted that he was no angel, but on this occasion, he was deeply hurt about what had been said, and was not going to let the matter drop. *"I would rather leave things in the boss's hands at the moment, but I* will say that this is the first time anything like this has ever happened to me." He added wryly: "*And I've had a fair bit of experience of referees. This is the most unusual experience of all. And it is not just me that is saying so. Other players heard what was going on.*"

Albert was right behind his teammate and more than willing to give him his support. "*I informed the referee that I would report him and I did – to Matt Busby at half time.*

"*I have never heard anything like it from a referee before. But at the moment I cannot say what I did hear. The matter is in the club's hands.*

"*At first, I thought he must be joking, it was so unusual. It all seemed so laughable. You wouldn't believe it if I told you some of the things I heard.*"

"*I heard everything that was said. But until I know what the club's decision is, I am saying nothing except that, if they want to take it any further, I'll be a witness.*"

The Referee's Association were firmly behind Pullin, but there was to be no quick decision on the matter and it would be mid-February before the Football Association dealt with the complaint, appointing a committee to look into the matter.

Over the course of two hours, the three man committee questioned the referee, Alex Jackson of West Bromwich Albion, Cliff Lloyd of the Players' Union, Matt Busby, Albion manager, Archie Macaulay and his chairman, Major Wilson Keys, Denis Law and Albert. They reached the conclusion that Pullin had made the alleged remarks to Law and was severely censured and warned about his future conduct.

Bill Rogers, secretary of the Referee's Association said that Pullin had "*left himself wide open somewhere,*" while the referee himself decided that like Albert's £45,000 transfer tag, the committee's decision would be with him wherever he went, so decided to resign as a League referee.

Manchester United still managed to keep their heads above water despite the 3-0 reversal at the Hawthorns. They were one of four clubs on nineteen points in the bottom half of the table and had a seven-point advantage over Leyton Orient, who already looked doomed, and were four better off than second bottom Fulham. It was, however, merely the halfway stage of the season.

Seven days later, the First Division programme was thrown into complete disarray, four games were postponed due to the weather, while United's home fixture against Arsenal was abandoned in the fifty-seventh minute with the Gunners winning 1-0, while Aston Villa's home match against Manchester City also failed to last the ninety minutes.

If Manchester United required some breathing space during this often-problematic season, then it came courtesy of the weather. The next fixture, a 1-0 victory on Boxing Day against Fulham, which saw Albert having his penalty kick saved by Macedo, was their last League outing until February 23rd as snow and ice brought the country to a standstill.

In the course of an ordinary season, March would have seen the league tables give an indication of how the season was going to pan out, while the FA Cup would be in full swing, with the semi-finals due to be played towards the end of that month. This season, however, Manchester United had still eighteen League fixtures to fulfil as March reared its head, while their FA Cup campaign had not even started.

The FA Cup in recent seasons had not brought anything to shout about around Old Trafford. There were defeats to lesser lights such as Norwich City and at the hands of Albert's former Sheffield Wednesday; although, the semi-final defeat at the hands of Tottenham Hotspur, the previous season, did give them the determination to go one step further this time around, whenever the competition finally got started.

Due to the postponements, the games would now be coming thick and fast and, two days after the league programme resumed on March 2nd with a 2-2 draw at Blackburn Rovers, Manchester United were off to Huddersfield Town for their FA Cup third round tie.

Within three minutes of the start, Albert had put United a goal in front and there was no looking back, as they went on to score five without reply.

The FA Cup was to prove a worthwhile distraction as league form was to be dismal, the enforced lay-off being of no help whatsoever, as only two of the next eleven fixtures, which took the season up to the beginning of May, were won, with seven of the eleven being defeats. The situation was serious. They were fourth bottom on twenty-nine points, one above Birmingham City and Manchester City. Leyton Orient remained anchored at the bottom, ten points adrift.

Cup-wise, however, it was all smiles, as, for some unknown reason, League form was edged to the side, forgotten for ninety minutes. A solitary goal from Albert, eight minutes before half time, was enough to knock out Aston Villa in round four.

Finding the competition to his liking, he turned in a man-of-the-match performance against Second Division leaders Chelsea, scoring United's second in their 2-1 win at Old Trafford in the fifth round tie, before finding the net again in the sixth round at Highfield Road against Coventry City as United marched to the semi-finals for the second consecutive season on the back of a 3-1 win.

Albert's goals would have been more than welcome in the First Division survival dog-fight, but they failed to materialise, and his goal-scoring FA Cup campaign also came to a halt in the semi-final tie against

Southampton, where a solitary goal divided the two sides, Denis Law's strike taking Manchester United to Wembley.

The semi-final was a game that Albert missed through injury as in the days prior to the fixture he had only given himself a 50/50 chance of playing, having bruised his thigh muscle again Wolves five days previously, and, as the tie drew nearer, he was to fail a late fitness test, much to his disappointment.

With Wembley having been reached, everything could be concentrated upon First Division survival in the twenty-four days prior to that date below the famous twin towers on May 25th, which was to see seven fixtures crammed into a space of twenty days.

Albert's league season had seen him play mainly in the number eight shirt, with the occasional outing in the number nine and number ten. Towards the end of April, however, he had been handed the red number seven shirt, only to switch to number nine as May beckoned. No matter what shirt he wore, he always gave 100%, although his goals contribution was to be nil, until the third-last game of the season.

Wednesday May 15th 1963 saw the sun rise in Manchester on a day that would prove monumental to both United and neighbours City. Maine Road had played host to countless memorable fixtures over the years, United having contributed to them in fairly recent times with those memorable mid-fifties European Cup ties when Old Trafford had no floodlights, but the ninety-minutes about to be played out at the Moss Side arena could be considered more important than those nights against foreign opposition. This was local rivalry, which would leave the loser staring Second Division football next season firmly in the face.

Manchester United had three games remaining and were on thirty-one points. Below them, Birmingham City had one game left and were also on thirty-one points. Then came Manchester City, who had two games left, sitting on thirty points.

On the eve of the Maine Road clash, Albert and his team mates were presented with mopeds at the Blackpool International Cycle and Motorcycle Show, happy to pose on their new mode of transport beneath the Blackpool tower, taking their minds, momentarily, away from the important ninety minutes on the horizon.

On the night of the derby confrontation, the streets around the Moss Side venue were swarming with supporters, so much so that the gates were locked by 7.00pm, half an hour before kick-off mainly due to a Kippax Street gate being forced open and many gaining 'free' admission.

With only eight minutes gone, Harley gave City the lead, and, in an ill-tempered match, it looked as though that solitary goal would be enough to secure both points for City and nudge United closer to Division Two.

But with only six minutes remaining, City goalkeeper Harry Dowd tangled with Denis Law, bringing the United forward down and despite the keeper being momentarily knocked out, the referee pointed to the penalty spot.

It was November 24th when Albert Quixall had last scored a league goal, two against Aston Villa, but he showed no hesitation in picking up the ball, placing it on the penalty spot and firing it past Dowd to virtually assure United of First Division safety and send City towards the Second Division. Arguably, it was the most important goal of his career.

Thankfully, the second-last fixture was against, already doomed, Leyton Orient, which was to end in a 3-1 victory, the 3-2 defeat at Nottingham Forest on the final day being meaningless as all eyes were now firmly focussed on Wembley five days later.

Although he missed out on the semi-final through injury, but returned in the number seven shirt for the final three league outings of the season, there was no guarantee that he would be in the starting line-up for the Wembley show piece.

Back in the day, playing in the FA Cup final in front of a packed Wembley crowd was every footballer's dream, one, however, that few achieved, so there was a sigh of relief when Matt Busby named his starting eleven and Albert was included.

If the trophy was won on transfer fees paid out, then United were the ready made winners, with Albert's £45,000 sitting alongside Denis Law's £115,000 and Pat Crerand's £50,000. The whole Leicester side hadn't cost as much as Law alone. Talent-wise, again, United edged themselves in front with the likes of Bobby Charlton and David Herd, another big money buy, but, on current form, it was Leicester City who were favourites to lift the trophy for the first time in their history.

On the day, however, there was always only going to be one winner.

Albert was the instigator of the first real United attack, hitting an inch-perfect cross-field pass to Charlton, but he was dispossessed by Riley. Soon afterwards, Albert, having taken on a more attacking position, was only inches away from being put through by Law. He was also the first to trouble Banks in the Leicester City goal, his free kick being firmly held by the England keeper. The keeper had to again be at his best when an Albert-Law move set David Herd through, but his low shot was easily saved.

Combining once again with Denis Law, Albert saw his shot saved by Banks, but the keeper's throw out to McLintock saw the Leicester half-back dispossessed by Crerand who moved forward before passing to an unmarked Law who sent a low shot past Banks to put United in front.

Along with Law, Albert was a constant thorn in the Leicester side and David Herd made it 2-0 in the fifty-sixth minute and, just after the hour mark, Albert almost made it three, but his twenty-yard effort was saved by Banks.

Leicester managed to pull a goal back with ten minutes remaining through Keyworth when United failed to clear an indirect free kick, awarded against Gaskell for time-wasting, but there was to be no fight-back, as five minutes later, David Herd claimed his second of the afternoon to give Manchester United a comfortable 3-1 victory.

Comfortable it certainly was, with Albert describing the victory as: *"Like a Tuesday morning training practice. They left so many open spaces; it was just like moving around Old Trafford. We just couldn't go wrong."*

CHAPTER SEVEN
ALL THAT GLITTERS IS NOT GOLD

With the FA Cup safely locked away in the Old Trafford boardroom, United headed off on a short tour of Italy, but, upon returning home, Albert spent the remainder of the close season playing golf and cricket, before returning to action on Wednesday August 7th at Hampden Park, Glasgow, facing a Glasgow Select side in a charity game that was lost 2-1.

It was little more than a polished up friendly, as was the FA Charity Shield fixture against First Division champions Everton, at Goodison Park ten days later. However, the 4-0 defeat on Merseyside was to come at a price. A heavy one at that.

Albert's contribution in that 4-0 defeat was no more or no less than that of any of his teammates, but Matt Busby decided to wield the axe for the opening First Division fixture against Sheffield Wednesday at Hillsborough and there was no return visit to his old stomping ground for Albert, as he found himself omitted from the side, as did Johnny Giles and David Herd. David Gaskell was another change in personnel, but his was enforced through injury. A poor performance in a 2-1 defeat against Eintracht Frankfurt had also convinced Busby that the name Quixall should be omitted from his starting eleven.

The reaction to being demoted to Manchester United's Central League side was immediate: "United Stars Want Move" claimed the Saturday morning newspapers on the opening day of the 1963-64 season, with both Albert and Johnny Giles unhappy at being dropped.

If the reaction by the disgruntled duo to being dropped was quick, then equally quick was the Manchester United board's decision to put both players on the transfer list, with the *Manchester Evening News* of

Tuesday August 27th, not only announcing their availability, but the fact that Celtic could well be interested in signing both individuals, although a move to Scotland might not be something that they would consider, while their transfer fees could well be beyond the means of the Parkhead club.

There was obvious interest in the pair, but Stoke City manager Tony Waddington, who had expressed an interest in taking him to the Potteries less than a year previously, perhaps sounded the warning bells to any club considering signing Albert, saying: *"He has a heap of talent, but, much as I would like him, I will not bid because he is a player who apparently is not prepared to be dropped."*

If clubs were indeed holding off on approaches for Albert, Johnny Giles secured a move away from Old Trafford without a problem, signing for Leeds United for £33,000 before August had disappeared from the calendar.

Albert, however, had to kick his heels in the Manchester United Central League side, as Busby's selected eleven got their 1963-64 campaign off to a favourable start with four wins and two draws in their opening half dozen games, scoring twenty-one goals in the process.

Rumours of interest from Italy began to surface, with *Corriere dello Sport* saying that he had been offered to Lazio *"on a very satisfactory basis,"* with a fee of around £42,000 mentioned, while Genoa were also rumoured to be interested. But even although he was disgruntled by the whole situation, Albert added: *"with two years' contract behind me, I can afford to take my time."*

Even two consecutive defeats in mid-to-late September couldn't bring Albert in from the cold, while a sending off playing against Manchester City's second string at Old Trafford on October 2nd, for kicking an opponent, leading to a suspension, would have done his cause little good. However, there was to be something of a surprise recall to first team action in the European Cup Winners Cup first round second-leg tie against Dutch side Willem II at Old Trafford on October 15th.

Having drawn the first leg in Rotterdam 1-1, Busby perhaps favoured experience over youthful exuberance in this starting line-up, hence the recall, but, whilst unable to find the net in the 6-1 victory, he enjoyed a favourable return to the big stage, showing much in the way of determination. It had, however, to be taken into consideration that this was Second Division opposition that they were up against.

Nevertheless, Albert's performance over the ninety minutes was enough to see him keep his place for the visit to the City Ground, Nottingham, four days later. Albert scored in United's 2-1 victory, but his seven-day suspension after the sending-off in the reserve's match against Manchester City, meant that he missed the next home fixture against West Ham United.

On previous form, missing a game could have seen him back in the Central League side, his place taken by a teammate, but, brought in from the cold by Matt Busby, he was given a continued opportunity to redeem his previous indiscretions and was back in the starting line-up to face Blackburn Rovers at Old Trafford on October 28th. The 1-0 defeat at Old Trafford in the previous fixture, United's first reversal in five games, perhaps helping his cause.

Despite having scored five goals, playing in three different positions, it was centre forward David Herd who made way for Albert's return and, although the number nine jersey wasn't totally unfamiliar, it was a position that he had not filled since the previous May.

Unperturbed by the relatively alien position, he was to notch the equaliser for United within thirty seconds of Blackburn taking a fourth minute lead, before scoring a second just before half time to give Manchester United a 2-1 lead. A lead that they were to relinquish and share the points in a 2-2 draw.

There was no case for dropping him now and despite defeats against Aston Villa and Liverpool, having moved back to a more familiar outside right spot, he enjoyed an eight-game run in the first team. That, however, was to come to an end in early December as an injury in the 4-1 European Cup Winners Cup second leg tie against Tottenham Hotspur at Old Trafford on December 10th, saw him missing the home fixture against Sheffield Wednesday and against Everton at Goodison Park.

The Goodison Park side repeated their Charity Shield victory, again winning 4-0. Albert, passing a fitness test, Matt Busby was more than happy to restore him to his starting eleven to face near neighbours Burnley on Boxing Day.

Despite David Herd equalising Burnley's seventh-minute opener, United were simply brushed aside by the effervescent claret and blue shirts, going on to lose 6-1. Pat Crerand's sending off making no difference whatsoever.

Forty-eight hours later, when Burnley visited Old Trafford for the return fixture, they were hammered 5-1 by an Albert Quixall-less Manchester United, Busby handing the number seven shirt to a scrawny Irish waif called George Best. Unknown at the time, Albert Quixall had played his last first team game for Manchester United.

Whilst Albert kicked his heels in Manchester United's Central League side, where quotes such as *"his touches of class were often in evidence,"* the

United first team would lose only two of their next dozen First Division fixtures, following that 5-1 thrashing of Burnley, but of more concern was the 5-0 defeat in Portugal against Sporting Club Lisbon, having won the first-leg at Old Trafford 4-1. Even that shattering European Cup Winners Cup quarter-final defeat, coupled with three consecutive draws in March, could not bring Albert in from the cold. Problems with a knee injury did little to help his cause.

As the curtains came down on the 1963-64 season, it was decided that a cartilage operation was required if Albert was to see a return to first team football, as the knee injury had been troubling him for some time. But having come through the operation without any problems and returning to training, there was no re-call. Being named as twelfth man was the closest he could get.

Rumours of transfer interest from Hull City were swiftly denied by their management team, but with the new season only three weeks old, Albert was packing his boots and saying his goodbyes to everyone at Old Trafford, moving a few miles up the road to Oldham Athletic in what was a move that surprised everyone.

"*Latics May Go For Quixall*" was squeezed into a small sidebar on the front of the *Manchester Evening News* of Monday September 7th, while in the same newspaper, twenty-four hours later, his transfer was confirmed in a mere seventeen words: "*Albert Quixall signed for Oldham Athletic late this afternoon after talking over terms with manager Les McDowell.*"

The shine of the one-time 'Golden Boy of British Football' had long since faded and the £45,000 transfer fee had diminished to a mere £7,000. Breaking it down further, his 179 first team outings with Manchester United, playing for what would have been a minimum £20 per week, coupled with his transfer fee, worked out at around £450 per game. His 40 Central League outings would lower that figure only slightly. *"It's all a little sad and sobering,"* wrote Peter Lorenzo in the *Daily*

Herald, "But as little Albert moves down, he leaves behind a stern warning for the hundreds of starry-eyed youngsters who dream of reaching for the Soccer stars.

"The warning: there is no guaranteed path to success."

Mentioning his transfer to Manchester United, Lorenzo added: *"The Golden Boy couldn't fall. But he did.*

"Let this unhappy story be a lesson and a challenge to all other would-be golden boys in the game today."

The drop from the First Division to the Third was one that few would have contemplated, it is certainly not one that Albert Quixall would have been linked with, the difference between Boundary Park and Trafford Park being incomparable. But it was September, not April 1st.

"I'm looking forward to playing with Oldham and consider it a new challenge," Albert said following the move. *"It may take me a couple of games to settle in but I will do my best to help them regain some of their former success."*

It had been a mere six years, almost six years to the day since he left Sheffield Wednesday and crossed the Pennines to join Manchester United. Six years that had promised so much for both club and player.

He had been Matt Busby's 'marquee' signing in the wake of the Munich disaster, a cornerstone upon which to rebuild the shattered club. Here was a hugely talented individual and a player ideally suited for a club of the calibre of Manchester United.

It was a transfer that should have seen the player re-establish himself in the England international set-up, whilst confirming his status as the 'Golden Boy Of British Football'. So, where did it all go wrong for this precocious talent?

He perhaps arrived at Old Trafford at the wrong time. September 1958 was a mere seven months after Munich, the scars hadn't healed, the re-building would be a long drawn-out affair and perhaps too much was expected of Albert Quixall. The player himself, who was to admit that had it not been for knowing and being friends with Roger Byrne, Duncan Edwards and Tommy Taylor, he would never have joined Manchester United, so perhaps he put too much effort into attempting to restore the club to its former glories and maintain the legacy of his lost friends.

If he had a flaw in his make-up it was, as it had been at Sheffield Wednesday, the lack of goals, but, then again, a noted goal scorer he never was and few have the ability to be both makers and takers.

On his game, there were few better. His ability was unquestionable, but perhaps Busby, for all his expertise and ability to get the best out of his players, and remember, here was a man who had been knocking on death's door in the not too distant past, just didn't quite know how best to utilise his record signing.

But then again, perhaps it had nothing to do with Manchester United and Matt Busby, it could have been a case that Albert Quixall's star had shone too brightly in the sky too soon, as had been the case with his England international career and he did harbour the belief that during his early career, in particular whilst doing his national service, he was often playing four games per week, thinking nothing of it at the time, but in reflection could be considered as having had a lasting effect.

The fall from grace is no cryptic crossword, or mathematical puzzle, the clues are few and far between, if at all visible, but another angle to pursue is, was the problem Albert Quixall himself? In Sheffield, he was comfortable in his surroundings, he had grown up there, he was an accepted face around town, but suddenly he was saddled with that £45,000 price tag, he had a huge spotlight on him in his new adopted city. Despite his self-assurance with a ball at his feet, the rolled-up shorts, here was a quiet individual, who in latter years shunned the lime-light, so was the transfer to Manchester United too much and he hid behind a mask, despite having settled in to his new environment well, and more than happy to play in any position when asked. Perhaps those latter few words add extra weight to Busby's not knowing where best to play him.

No matter what, we will never know why that bright light dimmed so quickly.

Albert had little time to be accustomed to his new surroundings and to contemplate how his world had turned on its axis, as he was straight into action twenty-four hours after signing, lining up against Bournemouth at Dean Court. It was to be an impetuous, feisty baptism of overly robust challenges and trouble on the terracing, but, despite prompting the majority of the Oldham attacks, Albert, cheered on by his wife and seven-year-old son, Paul, couldn't conjure up a goal for his team mates and the game fizzled out goal-less.

If Oldham Athletic thought that the addition of Albert Quixall to their ranks would ensure instant success those thoughts were misconceived, as the 0-0 draw on the south coast was followed by a 2-0 defeat at the opposite end of the country against Carlisle United. "*Lacked drive and initiative*," was the opinion of one reporter who watched the game. The following ninety minutes, his home debut against Bournemouth, was to see his apparently lost confidence return, showing fight and skill in the 1-1 draw, watched by 13,000. It was, however, only momentary, as four days later, against Port Vale, again at Boundary Park, his contribution was considered: "*negligible, flashing in and out of the match like a sleight-of-hand performer, pushing out a pass here, taking a free kick there.*"

Two goals in the 2-2 draw with Colchester United boosted his confidence, but, not for the first time, he was to find himself on the treatment table with that recurring knee injury and it would be January 1965 before he would return to first team action, turning in a creditable performance on a snow-covered Boundary Park against Watford.

Missing more games than he played, coupled by that niggling knee injury, Albert Quixall was a frustrated individual and it was a frustration that bubbled over against Barnsley in mid-April when he was sent off in the thirty-second minute following a challenge on Johnny Byrne.

It wasn't the first time that Albert had made the long solitary walk to the dressing rooms, but reflecting on the match he said: "*I am thinking over the position very seriously, but will not make up my mind until I see a copy of the referee's report.*

"*There was nothing wrong when Johnny Byrne went down in a tackle, though the referee said he was cautioning me. Then, as I was walking away, he suddenly swung round, pointed to the dressing rooms and said I had to go off. I have no idea what it for.*" The disciplinary hearing a couple of months later found him "guilty" of kicking Byrne and suspended him for fourteen days.

As April drew to a close, Albert had had enough and decided that he had had enough of Oldham and asked for a transfer, which was immediately agreed to by the Boundary Park board, perhaps deciding to cut their losses, due to him only playing in fourteen games following his transfer.

If Oldham Athletic had been considered a few steps down the ladder, then there were few rungs left to encounter if a suggested move to Runcorn was to be believed. Then it was Crewe who were showing an interest, but Albert was going nowhere, as he was taken off the transfer list and was back in favour under new Oldham manager, Gordon Hurst. *"Quixall will be in the forward line somewhere* (against Tranmere Rovers in the Football League Cup), *but I have not yet made up my mind where it is best to play him."* Back in the groove and having served his fourteen-day suspension, Albert returned to the fray in that game against Tranmere Rovers at Boundary Park on September 1st 1965.

The 3-2 scoreline, in Oldham's favour reads as though it was a close encounter, but in reality, Tranmere's two goals came towards the end, as the home side took their foot off the pedal, with Albert having run the show from start to finish. *"Their general"* was how the *Liverpool Daily Post* reporter saw him, adding that he: *"tore the Tranmere defence to ribbons."* He even managed a goal, Oldham's second, in the 38th minute.

Ten days later, having missed the solitary goal defeat against Millwall due to his knee trouble, Albert was on the score sheet again, notching a couple of goals, one from the penalty spot, against Gillingham in a 5-3 victory, with the press once again complimentary: *"The former Manchester United man has got the measure of lower grade soccer and paces it beautifully.*

"He showed everybody else how to do things by the ice cool way in which he scored from the spot to send Oldham on their way. Then he was continually splitting the Gillingham defence with slide rule passes to first one wing and then the other."

Saturday October 23rd saw Oldham up against Brentford and with the game only minutes old, and Brentford's Barry Thornley out to make his mark, a clash between the pair saw Albert collapse before the referee could even register a warning to either player. Recovering, Albert limped onto the wing, but was to collapse again and was carried off.

The injury, a trapped nerve, quickly healed and he was back in action the following Saturday, scoring from the penalty spot in the 2-0 victory over Bristol Rovers. A goal in the 2-2 draw against York City followed and it was beginning to look as though Albert was back in a comfortable environment, dictating the play and scoring goals, but just as the sun was beginning to shine brightly high in the sky, those dark, foreboding clouds suddenly reappeared.

On the coach journey to Mansfield for an FA Cup tie on November 13th, he took ill, then a month later he was to find his place in the Oldham starting eleven in jeopardy, following the £33,000 outlay for new signings: inside forwards, Dennis Stevens and Reg Blore, and centre forward, Frank Large, with rumours of another couple of signings more than possible before the end of the year.

"*And all this poses the question: what happens to Albert Quixall, one-time £45,000 golden boy? He cost Latics £7,000 when he came from Manchester United a year ago, and it looks as if he will be forced into the reserves unless they try and switch him to an attacking wing-half*" wrote Eric Thornton in the *Manchester Evening News*.

Missing from the Oldham line-up for the first fixture of 1966 against Shrewsbury Town, the 1-0 defeat forced the Oldham management into something of a re-think and Albert found himself back in the side to face Brentford on January 15th, retaining his place for the FA Cup tie against West Ham United the following week.

It was a glamour tie for the Boundary Park side and one that might well have given Albert sleepless nights, or at least made him reflect on when such opposition was part and parcel of his life at the top of the footballing tree.

As it was, he had done enough against Brentford to ensure his place in the Oldham side to face the Hammers at Boundary Park, but the fixture must have released a few butterflies in his stomach, as he uncharacteristically missed from the penalty spot.

On another day, it might have had a telling effect on his performance, but on that cold January afternoon, Albert relished the taste of big-time football once again and turned in a man-of-the-match performance.

If you had not been at the match, or if you were to read the *Sunday Post* brief summary of the ninety minutes, then you would have been led to believe that Albert made amends for that penalty miss by scoring the equaliser: "*In the 79th minute he trapped a long centre, flicked the ball in the air and beat Standen with an overhead kick.*" Only problem was that it was Blore who scored.

An injury against Mansfield in late February caused no prolonged stay on the sidelines as he soon recovered, but the words 'Quixall' and 'injury' were now becoming perhaps too frequently spoken in the same breath and this could well have been something that was to see his name linked with a managerial appointment in early March.

In a search for a new manager, Welsh League Division One side Pwllheli were rumoured to be looking at either John Charles or Albert to fill the vacant post and, with Oldham staring relegation from the Third Division in the face, it was perhaps something that would have appealed to him.

Due to Oldham's recent influx of new signings, and despite Albert's experience, he was to find himself demoted to the half-back line from his normal front lying position. Although somewhat alien to him, he gave it his best shot, but it often wasn't good enough and he struggled to make any impression.

As the 1965-66 season drew to a close it would have become obvious to Albert and the Oldham support, that his days at the club were drawing to a close and it therefore came as no surprise when he was given a free transfer by the Boundary Park club, who had managed to hold onto their Third Division status by the skin of their teeth, or to be more exact, by one point.

So, Albert Quixall was without a club two years down the line from being released by Manchester United and as he pondered his future, it was a former Manchester City star who offered him the opportunity to continue playing, albeit having to take a further step down the footballing ladder and into the fourth tier of the English game.

"*Do you fancy coming to Stockport?*" was the question posed by the County manager and former Manchester City legend Bert Trautmann and he was given a positive response, with Albert signing for the Edgeley Park side. "*I want to make a fresh start and I think I will enjoy it here. There is a good set-up, with lots of potential,*" he was to say after signing on the dotted line.

"Quixall's Fourth Test" was the headline in the *Manchester Evening News* of Thursday August 18th 1966, as Dennis Stokoe turned the spotlight on County's new signing, who it was said was looking for glory again.

Some eighteen years previously, Albert had run out onto the Edgeley Park pitch, a slightly built, blond, Sheffield schoolboy, playing for 'The Possibles' against 'The Probables' in an England schools' trial and, looking back, he told Stokoe: "*I've never forgotten that trial match at Edgeley. Stockport has held happy memories for me ever since that day. It's a ground with a great atmosphere.*"

Albert, however, was now a thirty-two-year-old, a far cry from those care-free schoolboy days, when the sky was his limit and he had the footballing world at his feet. He now had to prove that the skill that took him to international recognition and that big-money move to Manchester United was still there, although to a lesser degree, while having also to prove to his critics that he was not injury prone and finished. An equally daunting task.

Although not bitter about his fall from Manchester United to Stockport County via Oldham, he did say about his time at Boundary Park: "*As it turned out, going to Oldham was a bad move. But how was I to know that at the time?*

"*I was there eighteen months and during the first season played only about twelve games because of a ligament injury behind the left knee.*

"*Then the following season I missed the first four matches* (through suspension). *This pegs you back and I just don't think I had time or luck to become adjusted to the different game I had to play.*

"*Coming to Stockport means many things to me. Eddie Quigley, the team manager, was my idol when I first started playing. I was in the Army with the trainer, Jimmy Meadows, and Bert Trautmann, our general manager, was a great player.*"

Stokoe reported that Albert looked fit and that he was of his future, but only time would tell.

Early signs were positive, converting a penalty and inspiring a County fight-back against Chester in a pre-1966-67 season Friendly Shield fixture at Edgeley Park, which was won 3-2 after being 2-1 behind.

With Albert Quixall in the ranks, alongside another 'veteran' in Len Allchurch, the former Welsh international and County's most expensive signing, Stockport County got off to an ideal start to their 1966-67 Third Division campaign, winning five of their opening six fixtures and drawing the other, results that propelled them to the top of the table. Those results had an added incentive for Albert and his team mates, as those victories brought improved attendances, which in turn supplemented the weekly wage packet, as they were on a crowd bonus of £2 per thousand spectators over 8,000.

Albert, however, was to miss two of those half dozen fixtures, having aggravated his knee injury against Chesterfield in early September, returning to the fray in mid-October, but it was becoming obvious to many observers that despite returning to first team football that the persistent knee problem was not going to go away anytime soon and he was soon back on the side lines.

Although still young at heart and capable of playing at Stockport's level, had his fitness level allowed, Albert had to finally admit that he could no longer fulfil his obligations to the club and, in early March, he announced that he was hanging up his boots, having played only thirteen first team games and five at reserve team level this season.

Although, it had been unlucky thirteen for Albert, he could take credit in having played a part, albeit a minor one, as Stockport won promotion to the Second Division, as champions at the end of that 1966-67 season.

Retirement, however, was simply from the professional game, as with a handful of weeks following his announcement, he was taking them out of the cupboard, giving them a polish and pulling them on again as a member of the T.V. Stars XI to face a Knutsford side in a charity match, lining up alongside three other former United notables in Johnny Morris, Stan Pearson and Charlie Mitten. Such fixtures would become a regular feature in Albert's diary.

The compensation he received upon giving up the game was certainly not enough to keep the wolf from the door, and, as he looked elsewhere to earn a living, he made the decision to go into the scrap metal business with Freddie Pye, another footballing hopeful who had enjoyed a very limited association with Manchester United as a youngster, with adverts in the *Manchester Evening News* in early August 1967 announcing the opening of their premises on Shrewsbury Street, Brooks's Bar, Moss Side. "METALS! METALS! METALS! – TOP PRICES GUARANTEED FOR ALL GRADES OF METALS – a subsidiary of Fred Pye Metal Merchants."

The partnership of Pye and Quixall was soon to extend beyond the scrap metal business, due to the former's position as manager of Cheshire League Altrincham, as he managed to coax his business partner to forget the charity kickabouts and turn out for Altrincham, whose ranks were being depleted by injuries and suspensions.

"*I have watched Albert play in charity matches on several Sundays,*" said Pye, "*and he seems to have recovered completely from his leg injury.*

"He is my best pal – and what are pals for? He's helping me out of a nasty spot. Right now, we're over a barrel."

In reply, Albert said: *"I am playing for nothing. It's only a short-term policy to help Fred out and normally I would have liked to do some more training, but they are in a terrible spot."*

Making his debut for Altrincham against Rhyl at centre forward, he displayed many of his old attributes, helping his team to a 4-3 victory, but it wasn't all going to be plain sailing, as, while playing for Altrincham's reserve side against Manchester Northern, he was given his marching orders during a 1-1 draw, picking up a fourteen-day ban in the process

As well as helping out on the playing side, Albert was persuaded to take on a coaching role, but he was soon to decide that his playing would simply be nothing more than appearances with other former professionals, TV stars and Pop Stars. Being outshone by Freddie Garrity, the front man of Freddie and the Dreamers, and no mean footballer, was enough to ensure that there would be no more comebacks in the professional game and hence the curtain finally came down on the career of a player who, as a youngster, had the world at his feet, but whose career nose-dived rapidly, with an early burn-out or injuries being the given reasons. Albert, however, never voiced his regrets.

CHAPTER EIGHT
THOSE TWILIGHT YEARS

The name Albert Quixall continued to spring up with much regularity in the nation's sports pages, almost a weekly feature in the *Green 'Un* as readers wanted questions on his career answered, or when the paper took a nostalgic look back on Wednesday's history, or in a reader's letter. One such letter appearing in January 1970, entitled "Quixall At His Greatest":
"The best goal I have ever seen was a superb piece of juggling by that great ball artist Albert Quixall in the Owls-Bristol City match. "With the score level, Albert received the ball on his head on the halfway line and must have run about 40 yards with the ball still on his head past the bewildered Bristol defenders. He then let the ball drop and thumped it into the net on the volley.

"*I wonder whether any other Green 'Un readers remember this goal. I doubt whether I shall ever see such a fantastic goal again.*

K. Angus, Rose Bank, Evesham, Worcs."

The sum of £45,000 was never far away and would have earned Albert a fair amount over the years if he had owned the copyright to it. There was also, of course, those match reports of the charity games where he made a guest appearance.

From time to time, he was also sought out for an interview, having been there, seen it and done it. In one such interview at the age of forty, in 1974, he gave his opinion on the current England international set up and also the money that was now in the game, saying that he didn't look back on the past out of disenchantment, "*I would never knock the game. One paper asked me to stir up trouble at United when I left. They offered me £3,000 for a story, but I wouldn't do anything to harm the game or Manchester United.*"

As regards United, they were never far from his thoughts and this writer remembers seeing him regularly at Old Trafford on a match day in the seventies, not making his way to a seat in the main stand, or the director's box, but sitting on the trainer's bench, beside the tunnel.

Life, however, was not a bed of roses for Albert and his family, as he lost all his savings in what he called "*a bad business venture,*" forcing him to work as a labourer in a Hillgate scrapyard. "*Fortunately, I had the good sense to buy my home from my soccer earnings. The rest was blown in a business venture which went completely wrong.*

"*Money is not my master. I am quite happy as I am.*

"*I've done everything that is to be done in football. I've captained a great team, won the FA Cup, England, travelled all over the world and been in the company of royalty. There are not a lot of people who have done all that. I'm complete I bear no* envy for wealth. I've never had a lot of money but it was never really important to me. Glory was what counted."

Hitting the age of sixty, all Albert Quixall had left were his memories and his family, as break-in at the family home in Stretford, Manchester saw Jeannette Quixall's cherished bracelet which had been made to include his Second Division Championship medal and FA Cup winners medal, was stolen in 1987. His England caps were sold at auction in 1993.

Although still a handful of years off pension age, Albert had been forced to retire from working at the scrapyard through ill-health in 1992 and had been living on £95 per week invalidity benefit. The ligament damage that took a toll on his playing career also prevented him from continuing to play golf, a game he loved which had seen him with a handicap of two.

Looking back, he was to say: *"I should have had something done with the knee all those years ago, but we didn't have the medical technology then.*

"The injury meant that I was forced to pack it in, in 1967. I played a few games for Stockport after United, but I was thirty-four and shouldn't really have carried on."

He was, however, far from being a forgotten figure at both Hillsborough and Old Trafford, but despite being invited to numerous dinners, reunions and games, he kept his distance. *"I'm not a recluse or anything like that. I could go to a lot of functions if I wanted, but I don't want to give the impression that I'm begging."* There was also the offer of a seat in the director's box at Hillsborough for life, but again, the offer was turned down. *"That's fantastic, but I couldn't really accept."*

Had it been in the modern era, besides having earned a fortune from the game itself, Albert Quixall, no matter what he said back in 1994, would have been a regular in the hospitality lounges at Old Trafford, recalling the tales of his career to an appreciative audience and a regular feature on the club's television channel, but he didn't curse his luck and think "if only." He enjoyed his time at the top and looked back with no real regrets.

He certainly wasn't a 'forgotten hero', as previously mentioned, his name would often crop up in various newspapers, with one such mention appearing in September 1995 in an interview with the then Derby County manager Jim Smith in a *Derby Daily Telegraph* article entitled 'My Favourite Player'. Smith wrote: *"Albert Quixall was an inside forward who played for England at one time. I was a Sheffield Wednesdayite and as a teenager I watched him from the Kop at Hillsborough*

"I would usually be playing for my school in the morning and then I'd have to dash home get changed and go to the match.

"He stood out even more because he was the first player to wear short shorts rather than the old long and baggy ones.

"He had tremendous ability and tremendous skill. I used to wish I could be like him.

"He was an all-round quality player, but I always remember one particular skill of his. "A goalkeeper – I forget which team – kicked the ball high in the air and it was coming down on the halfway line. Albert controlled it on his knee and took it past an opponent in the next movement. Brilliant.

"He was superb at taking penalties as well – he used to just slide them inside the post and into the back of the net.

"To me he was an outstanding player. Kenny Dalglish was probably in a similar mould and the nearest I have seen to him since.

"Albert was sold to Manchester United for £45000 and that was the biggest fee ever at the time In today's market he would be up there worth five or six or seven million pounds.

"His sister used to work with my mother in the Co-op in Sheffield, but I never met him until 1991 when Wednesday played Manchester United in the League Cup final.

"I went to a reception afterwards and he was there with Ron Springett Wednesday's old goalkeeper. I knew Ron so I went up to talk to them. There was still a feeling of awe to be actually speaking to him. I was very honoured. He even said he'd always wanted to meet me because of the nice things I'd said about him in pieces like this!"

Like many others who plied their trade on the mud churned pitches of the fifties and sixties, Albert's latter years were not to be spent in happy retirement with his family and friends, as he was to spend some twenty years in a care home suffering from dementia.

"Everything about him went," said his son Paul. *"His face, everything. He used to have good legs. I lifted the bed sheets up and they were just withered, like little pipe cleaners. It was very sad to see him in that condition.*

"It's like being in prison, but in your own body. He didn't recognise anybody. The television was on and he was staring at it but you could tell nothing was going in. It was too upsetting."

It was November 12th 2020 when the full-time whistle finally blew for Albert Quixall. He was eighty-seven. His final years had been far from pleasant for both Albert and his family. Like many professional footballers from his generation, he was to miss out on the riches and medical assistance that is available to those of the present day, but will those same individuals be remembered, respected and lauded as Albert and his colleagues were? It is very doubtful.

So, we come to the end of the Albert Quixall story, the one-time golden boy of British football, a career that is difficult to evaluate today. The importance of Albert Quixall as a Manchester United player hasn't been so much forgotten, more simply not recognised. His arrival in September 1958 came seven months after Munich. Manchester United were still in a state of inertia. Jimmy Murphy had managed to reconstruct a team that managed to reach the FA Cup final on a wave of emotion along with pure grit and determination while Matt Busby recovered physically and mentally. However, when the serious matter of rebuilding the decimated team got underway, it was towards Albert Quixall the net was cast and, to ensure he became a Manchester United player, that record-breaking fee was paid out.

Experience was a vital necessity on the CV's of players that Busby wanted in his rebuilding plans and that was certainly a box that Albert Quixall ticked. Although meteoritic, his career had sometimes stuttered, especially on the goals-front, but in his latter Hillsborough days, he had shown both leadership and the ability to find the net on a regular basis.

Having arrived at Old Trafford, he had the knowledge in abundance to pass on to the young players whose careers had been quickened at an unaccustomed pace. Whilst at the same time he was able to bring out the best in the likes of Bobby Charlton and Denis Violett and, at a later date, helping Pat Crerand, Denis Law and David Herd.

He had endured relegation battles in the past, so his experience a few years after having joined United when it was back to the wall stuff of the 1962-63 season was also invaluable. That same season also saw him play an important role in the march to the FA Cup final, a victory that, although not instantly, kick-started the sixties supremacy at home and abroad.

Had it not been for Manchester United's multi-productive youth policy, there is every possibility that Albert Quixall would have arrived at the club sooner as he was the type of player Matt Busby loved – a player with talent and flare, an entertainer, a maverick. It could be said that he was one who escaped United's clutches, but it could also be said that it would have been a lost cause as he was in the clutches of Sheffield Wednesday from a young age.

On the international stage, was Albert Quixall a failure, and were his lack of goals and later injuries the fault of Sheffield Wednesday, trying to get him to run before he could walk? We will never know.

There was no denying that Albert Quixall had the ability to become a first-class footballer, but there were two things that hung around his neck along with that never-to-go-away £45,000 price tag and they were his lack of goals and his performances in the white of England that saw him win a mere five international caps.

As regards goals, although not as technical as today's game, players still had to adhere to their manager's advice and play to his required systems, although, unlike the modern game, individuality and freedom of expression was not exactly frowned upon.

Perhaps Albert Quixall was asked to play a deeper role in the Sheffield Wednesday team. Concentrate on getting the ball to teammates who were more skilled and experienced in putting the ball in the back of the net. There was also the added pressure of Wednesday yo-yoing league form.

Some seven decades down the line, one can only offer an opinion on the shortage of goals and his inept ninety minutes on the international stage.

In respect of his international performances, again there may well have been multiple reasons behind this. Here was a young player, confident in his own ability, but barely out of his teens, thrown into an environment awash with seasoned professionals. Paired alongside the likes of, let's say, the elder statesmen of Finney and Matthews, he had every reason to be overawed. Perhaps they did find Albert not to their liking, perhaps they had informed him, in no uncertain terms, just how they wanted the ball played to them, failing to accept anything different. There might also have been the possibility of being asked to perform a different role than normal, something that even a player longer in the tooth would have needed more time to adjust to. Perhaps also, he was thrown into the international arena just that little bit too early, simply to pacify the cries for his inclusion from the sports pages of the national press.

As for those selectors who sat behind closed doors, they may have judged the Sheffield Wednesday youngster as another of those rebellious teenage, early twenties, males who thumbed their nose at authority, who wanted to be different and failed to conform with their straightlaced pre-World War Two beliefs. Football's answer to individuals such as pop music's Elvis Presley or Billy Fury, or the big screen idol in James Dean. Loved by many, but found distasteful by others. Who knows?

Albert Quixall could be debated long into the night, but today, he will be an unknown to the vast majority who pass through the Old Trafford turnstiles on a match day – a diminishing few will have seen him play. To others he is nothing more than a name in the history of Manchester United Football Club, a member of the 1963 FA Cup winning team, which is unfortunate, as he deserves more. More than that solitary medal with Manchester United, a Second Division championship won with Sheffield Wednesday and that handful of England Caps. None of which his family have to remember him by.

He was most definitely a player before his time. A brilliant footballer who deserved so much more and the first 'Golden Boy Of British football'.

However, there is something of an unusual postscript…

There were countless others who were captivated by the numerous talents of Albert Quixall, including race horse breeders Ted and Joy Caine who named one of their horses 'Quixall Crossett.' Unfortunately, his was no Shergar or Red Rum, this was the Eddie the Eagle of the horse racing world.

Trained by Middlesbrough pig-farmer Ted Caine, 'Quixall Crossett' (the Crossett part of the name coming from Caine's High Crossett farm) was a horse to be ignored when it came to serious betting, but he captivated the imagination of many who, knowing only too well that it had less than an outside chance of winning, would often bet a meagre amount in the hope that perhaps dame fortune would for once smile on the horse that its trainer said of in an 1999 interview: *"He enjoys himself, he just loves going racing. And even though he gets behind in most of the races, he carries on at his own pace, whereas the majority of horses would just grind to a halt.*

"He doesn't get in anyone's way and it would be a pity to retire him. I don't think the old boy would be able to cope with just standing out in a field with nothing to do."

Entering his first race in February 1990, when he finished eighteenth out of nineteen runners, he moved from flat racing to hurdles then onto chases with no real success, other than an odd second or third placing. That first past the post honour was never to be achieved.

In all, he had 103 consecutive defeats, beaten by eighty lengths in one race, but sadly, at the age of twenty-one, suffering from a couple of health problems, he was euthanised. His record for consecutive losses standing until 2021.

CHAPTER NINE
MY DAD

The name Albert Quixall will be forever etched into the histories of Sheffield Wednesday and Manchester United football clubs and he will always be remembered by those who were fortunate enough to have seen him play, either in the blue and white of the Yorkshire side or the red of Matt Busby's team. The memories of those supporters, however, are not something that his son Paul can share.

"I didn't really become aware that he was a footballer, never mind a famous one, until he had left Manchester United and joined Oldham Athletic," recalled Paul. "I was a mere two-years-old when he was transferred from Sheffield Wednesday to Manchester United for that record fee, so obviously, I was far too young to be aware of what he did when he wasn't at home.

"It would have been good to have seen him play in his heyday, for either Sheffield Wednesday or Manchester United, but it wasn't until he left United and moved to Oldham Athletic that I first saw him in action. Oldham Athletic against Bournemouth it was. But when he signed for the Latics, he was past his best, if I have to be honest, as he had suffered a bad knee injury. Back then, operations took longer, as did the recovery process. Whilst at the same time, you didn't get the same treatment that you do today. If there had been, things may well have been completely different for him.

"I was born in Sheffield in 1957, but raised in Manchester after we had moved there in 1959 following his transfer, so his Sheffield Wednesday career is something that I have no knowledge of, while I was just a young boy during his Old Trafford days. I had little, or indeed, no idea just how good a player my dad was and it wasn't until later years that such a realisation set in."

But despite the knowledge that the man he knew as "dad" was something more than just a footballer, but rather an individual who was admired by thousands of football supporters, there was, perhaps surprisingly, little in the way of football interaction between the father and son.

"Even as I grew older, he didn't talk a lot about football at home. That poignant, immediate post-Munich game between Sheffield Wednesday and Manchester United was never mentioned, perhaps this was due to him knowing some of those United players who died in the crash, in particular the Yorkshire lads, Mark Jones, Tommy Taylor and David Pegg.

"There were a couple of things that I do remember him saying to me, both regarding individual players. When asked about the best player he ever played against, there was no hesitation in naming Duncan Edwards. He would say that whenever United played Sheffield Wednesday, Matt Busby always got Duncan to mark him out of the game. On those occasions he always said that he never got a kick.

"The other player was George Best. He said that George took his place in the side when he left Manchester United, but while he regarded Duncan Edwards as his most difficult opponent, George Best was undoubtedly the best player he had ever seen in his whole life, as he could do things with a ball that no-one else could. Mentioning that, you have got to remember what some of those pitches were like back then. Derby County's Baseball Ground for instance was little more than a mud bath in winter. Then there were the players of the period. Every team had their 'hard-men,' people like Norman Hunter, Ron Harris and Dave Mackay.

"These players today don't know they are born. They couldn't compete now."

Back then football was an entirely different sport and many players of the period must look on enviously at the astronomical amounts of money made in today's game and in certain ways, it was indeed something that Albert Quixall did regret. "Yes, he did," said Paul. "I remember him saying that he should have been a coach, but when he finally retired, he decided to go into business which was a mistake and he later regretted it. There were obviously thoughts of 'what might have been' had he been born in a different era, but..."

Having been signed by Manchester United, no-one wants to leave, something that has always applied and it was no different in Albert Quixall's case. "No, he didn't want to leave," admitted Paul, "but with his injuries and operations, he knew within himself that he wouldn't be the same player as he had been, making it difficult to play in the First Division, so yes, it was difficult for him at that point.

"But what also disappointed him was the fact that, not when he left, but in later years, United did nothing to help any of their old players, no after care or anything. He would go to an odd dinner, but not many, as he was disappointed that the club didn't do more for the older players.

"Despite that, and the money side of things, he had a good life, other than his later years of course. He had represented Sheffield Boys, Yorkshire Boys and England Boys and was capped by England at various levels. When he was growing up, the family home overlooked Hillsborough and he always said that he would play there one day.

"Unfortunately, the only thing that I have from his footballing career is a photograph of United's 1963 FA Cup winning side, as the family home was burgled many years ago and everything was stolen, caps, medals, the lot."

Paul Quixall, although a reasonable footballer, was never going to emulate his father as a footballer. "I had trials with Sheffield Wednesday and Manchester City and could hold my own at local level, but I wasn't anywhere near my dad's standard."

As regards the latter years of Albert Quixall's life, years that would prove to be a testing time for all concerned due to his his dementia, Paul was to say: "It was a difficult time for all the family. It was upsetting."

That disease, from which many players of Albert Quixall's generation suffer, and have suffered, along with the loss of his memorabilia remain difficult for his son, but Paul still manages a laugh when asked if he ever had a bet on that horse. "Oh yes," came the reply.

Paul Quixall can be proud of his father's achievements within the game and that he is still remembered today as the one-time 'Golden Boy of English Football.'

ACKNOWLEDGEMENTS

Many thanks to Paul Quixall for taking the time to talk to me about his father. Also to Terry Siddall for his help with the photographs

www.ingramcontent.com/pod-product-compliance
Lightning Source LLC
Chambersburg PA
CBHW052049070526
44584CB00017B/2111